I'm Too
Young
to Be
This Old

I'm Too Young to Be This Old

Poppy Smith

SPIRE

© 1997 by Patricia (Poppy) Smith

Published by Revell
a division of Baker Publishing Group
P.O. Box 6287, Grand Rapids, MI 49516-6287
www.revellbooks.com

Spire edition published 2009
ISBN 978-0-8007-8779-0

Originally published by Bethany House in 1997

Printed in the United States of America

Scripture is taken from the HOLY BIBLE, NEW INTERNATIONAL VERSION. NIV®. Copyright © 1973, 1978, 1984 by International Bible Society. Used by permission of Zondervan. All rights reserved.

To my husband, Jim,
and our two children, Malaika and Elliot.

Your interest in this project delights me.
I appreciate your sense of humor and
your willingness to let me write honestly
about life at our house.

Contents

1

What's Happening to Me?

"What are those things under my eyes?" I wailed, peering into the bathroom mirror.

"Festoons," Jim, my doctor-husband, pronounced matter-of-factly. Holding his razor in midair like a baton, he continued, "That's the medical term for those bags under your eyes. They happen to women your age."

"How sweet of you," I muttered, stalking out and leaving him grinning at his early morning humor.

Waking up and finding bags under my eyes no longer shocks me. I've learned to live with it. I also take seriously a bit of advice from an aging movie star—sleep sitting upright or, failing that, on your back with at least two pillows. When

I forget and sleep on my side, in the morning I discover that my face needs ironing.

Of course, other clues tell me something is happening to me. But like most emotionally healthy women, I try to ignore them. I'm amazed at how grown-up my children look. They're clearly too old to be mine! Something is wrong with my friends as well—they seem to be aging prematurely. And even though my husband is ten years older than I am, it scares me when he utters words like *retirement* and *home all day*.

Help! What's going on?

Actually, I know what's happening. I'm in the muddled middle years. I have joined the ranks of millions of forty- and fifty-something women who respond to aging by cunningly disguising gravity-prone figures and slathering on anti-wrinkle creams, enjoying a state of denial for as long as possible.

Recognize yourself here?

If you do, you are likely in what I call the *reluctant passage*, a season of life few women, if any, enter willingly.

When does this season begin? There's no particular birthday that, when reached, uniformly plunges a woman into midlife. We're as individual as our DNA. Most of us, however, sense changes taking place anytime from our late thirties to mid-forties.

Not long after I noticed these beginning signs, I frequently found myself deeply absorbed in thought, staring out of windows or gazing at blank walls. Often I'd drive without noticing where I was going, brooding about my life. *Had I made wise choices? Had I put God and my family first? Was I someone who could be useful in the years ahead?* The answers depended largely on my mood.

In my mind, I peered cautiously at what lay ahead, sensing the beginning of a long journey across a pivotal life-bridge. I couldn't imagine myself or anyone else my age crossing this bridge with giant, eager strides. Instead, I envisioned myself leaving youth's familiar territory and cautiously moving forward in a step-by-step exploration of the unknown.

The forties and fifties are a major turning point in life, taking us from the old age of youth into the youth of old age. We can't dig in our heels and say, "I'm not crossing over," nor can we detour around this part of our journey. We can, however, choose what attitude we will have about it.

Cringing at the Thought

Most of us cringe at the thought of entering mid-life. At least I did. We laugh at "over the hill" and "mid-life" jokes, so long as they are aimed at someone else. But we bristle when anyone implies we might be in any sort of crisis.

As we set foot on the reluctant passage we wonder if our marriage will hold together. Or if our children will stay in touch. Outdated stereotypes like "menopause makes you crazy," "life is over at forty," and "dress to suit your age" (why don't they just go ahead and say "dowdy"?) flash through our minds, causing fear and dread.

Thinking about the future can be fraught with questions: Will I be lonely? What about the dreams I still harbor—are they forever out of reach? Am I going to feel aimless—even useless? In the throes of these dark thoughts, aided by my bent for the dramatic, I began to visualize aging as a prelude to decay and dependence, ending in death. My overactive imagination left no room for God's promise to never leave us—to never leave *me*.

After a time of wallowing in the mid-life blues, I decided to look at the truth. Although an increasing number of marriages break up on the rocks of mid-life, the majority stay together.[1] Most children love their parents, despite occasional hot words to the contrary. They also keep in touch, though less often than we'd like.

Nor does life have to be lonely or aimless. By shedding outdated stereotypes of what you can and can't do in mid-life and daring to act on your dreams, the years ahead can be the richest you have known. As for decay, dependence, and death, the key to fulfilling years ahead lies in exchanging a mentality of doom and gloom for a spirit of hopefulness. Take care of your body, deepen your dependence on God, and don't die before your actual date of decease.

Instead of cringing at the thought of being in the reluctant passage, boldly grasp your new identity as a more mature, improved model of your younger self. True, the packaging is slightly wrinkled and maybe a bit lumpy, but what does that matter?

Well, let's be truthful. For some of us, it matters a great deal.

Accepting a New Identity

Because of the age difference between my husband and me, I've lived a long time with the illusion of being permanently young. When we went to parties or social events with people Jim's age, I always felt like the young wife of an older man.

Much as I wanted to hold on to my illusion, I've had to admit the truth. Being a "young wife" had become a figment of my imagination.

Letting go of my youthful identity and coming to grips with one less valued by our culture—"middle-aged wife"—didn't happen quickly or easily. Watching the effect that slim, alluring, eyelash-batting women twenty years my junior had on men, though, brought reality home. I realized few woman my age could hope to have the same impact. Musing about growing older, I began to wonder, *Maybe building a new sense of identity based on inner beauty would make aging easier to accept....*

Mid-life transition takes time. Driving across a bridge from the United States into Canada is an instant transition from one country to another. Moving from one perception of self to another is a slow process. For a while our eyes keep straying to life's rearview mirror. We are gripped by a sense of loss and a longing to go back in time.

Moving through this passage, strange and wild ideas came to me, like getting pregnant again. I thought a lot about the joys of having a chubby little baby cooing away in its crib. This image had powerful appeal until I thought of my adult children gasping, "You're WHAT?"

It's all right to look back and allow ourselves to experience feelings of loss, but eventually we have to look ahead or else miss the adventure God has waiting for us.

For some women, awareness and acceptance of the mid-life transition is like traversing gently rolling hills that gradually take us into an exciting new land. Some find the journey uncomfortable but manageable. Others feel like travelers trying to scale formidable mountains. As they face changes in status, roles, health, or finances, each step brings a new crisis.

Growing Through Crisis

My friend Becky saw her shaky twenty-eight-year marriage collapse when her oldest son married. He had been her emotional prop. After her husband divorced her, Becky careened from one catastrophe to another. She became a single mother with no money. Her deep hurts were made more painful by divided loyalties among her children and the loss of former friends. Her pastor told her to stop teaching Sunday school and singing in the choir. Becky survived these disastrous years by turning to God for help in her battle with hurt and resentment. Today she is discovering His fresh path for her life.

With God's help, crisis and change act like fertilizer—like growth-granules. Sprinkled on the ground of our mid-life years, they spur us to grow and blossom into the person God knows we can become.

Whatever the impact of our daily struggles, we confront numerous changes in this season of life. We also plunge into a wide-ranging assessment of our lives. We emerge, eventually, on the threshold of new horizons.

Face to Face With Change

Your Body . . . What's Next?

After age forty, my body seemed to take fiendish delight in presenting me with new problems on a regular basis. A line from an old hymn, "Change and decay in all around I see," became not a theological statement but daily reality.

Most obviously, mid-life brings physical changes. In the middle years, we not only go through menopause but our susceptibility to illnesses such as diabetes, heart disease, and cancer climbs. Seeing early warning signs of what could lie ahead, I've stopped lying in bed idly looking at my cross-country ski machine standing two steps away. For years, I had asked myself if I felt like exercising. My answer was no. Now, whether I feel like it or not, I haul myself out of bed and daily (well, almost daily) huff and puff my way to better health. (My slimmer hips are a great incentive, too.)

Your Memory

Some days you're sure your mind has lost a few computer chips. Don't worry. This is normal. Not only is your body changing but, it seems, so is your mind.

Not long ago, I was late for a meeting and hurriedly backed the car out of the driveway. Suddenly I thought, *Did I brush my teeth?* I couldn't remember! I quickly set the brake, dashed into the house, and brushed my teeth—just in case. And then I wondered, *What is happening to me?*

Walking into a room and wondering why I'm there or staring into the refrigerator and trying to remember what I'm looking for is all part of the package. All my best friends do it. So is swallowing a pill and five minutes later asking myself, *Did I or didn't I?*

Your Emotions

Your emotions are also apt to misbehave. Instead of sensibly taking orders from your brain, they decide to run wild and be uncooperative, like some petulant child.

Battling "the blues" is common. So is wondering *What is the matter with me?* because you cry at the least provocation. Your family is probably as baffled as you are by your emotional ups and downs. Be patient with yourself. Emotional swings are part of the muddled middle years.

Your Children

As if the changes *you* are experiencing weren't enough, your family is also changing. Your delightful little boy is now a strapping six-footer, hand extended for cash and stomach growling for food like a bear out of hibernation. When you weren't looking, the little girl you tearfully waved off to college may have boomeranged back and be cozily curled up in her old room.

Now, instead of confidently issuing time-honored "Mom" commands, you have to swallow what's on the tip of your tongue. Yes, you are their parent, but time has marched on. Whether their behavior affirms it or not, they are now adults.

Your Parents

With our parents living longer than ever before, long-distance conferences between siblings about what to do for Mom and Dad is a reality for many. So is criss-crossing the country racking up frequent flyer miles to give support, get the old homestead ready for sale, figure out finances, and persuade them to move into a safe environment.

Watching their decline and sensing the inevitable loss can be a wrenching part of the middle years. But by choosing to lovingly parent our parents, we have a special opportunity to return their devotion.

Your Marriage

If you are married, your perception of your spouse can also undergo a radical change. Some enchanted evening, you will look across your living room and see a stranger. Actually, it's the man you married. Out of nowhere the question will pop into your mind, *What happened to that amorous man I married? Who is this aging male snoring in the recliner?*

At the same time, your husband probably looks at you when he's in a more pensive mood and wonders, *What happened to her? Where is that cute little thing I married?* This, too, is normal.

Your View of Yourself

The most far-reaching changes are taking place in the unseen chambers of our minds. There, a slow yet unstoppable transformation occurs in our self-perception, erupting in questions that tumble out on top of one another in a demanding frenzy:

Who am I now that I've grown up?
What do I want to do with the rest of my life?
Is it all downhill from here?
How do I find meaning and purpose in the years ahead?

As both outer and inner changes carry us along, we plunge into the turbulent waters of assessing all we previously took for granted.

Plunged Into Assessment

Relationships

Mid-life produces a lot of self-examination. But it isn't navel-gazing. It's not wasted time.

Some singles wonder if they will be able to attract a man as the years take their toll.

Liz's husband left her with two small sons when she was in her early thirties. "I dread every birthday," she admits, "because the older I get the less likely I'll be to remarry." Facing reality isn't easy, but hiding from the truth would keep her from preparing for the future.

Marge, a would-be mom, anxiously questions her chances of conceiving and giving birth as her reproductive clock marches toward midnight.

As a menopausal wife, Jean wonders if she is losing interest in sex or if her husband will lose interest in her.

Like most mothers, Yvonne looks at her nearly adult children and asks, "Was I a good mom?"

Accomplishments

Whether we've spent our years in the home or in the workplace, we wonder if we have accomplished anything worthwhile and whether it's too late to begin something new.

At forty, when I left my teaching position with Bible Study Fellowship, the mid-life evaluation process hit me full force. Who was I now that my title and job description were gone? Did I still have value? Rattling around in my mind was the nagging question: *What am I going to do with the second half of my life? Run off to a tropical island? Find another occupation? Conquer academia? Aimlessly wander the malls?*

Purpose and Meaning

We mid-lifers resemble two-year-olds. In this ruminating state we badger our inner parent with endless questions, all beginning with WHY:

WHY am I doing what I'm doing?

WHY am I staying in this marriage, this friendship, this job?

WHY am I serving Thanksgiving dinner AGAIN?

WHY am I doing this for my church?

WHY am I doing this for my children?

WHY aren't I receiving any satisfaction or support?

Tell your two-year-old self to calm down. You are in a process and the answers will come.

Self-Awareness

Discovering who you are, now that you've grown up, is also part of working through the reluctant passage. You might be surprised at what you find.

Cocooned in my private chariot, I can safely indulge my passion for pounding music, turning up the car stereo as loud as my ears can stand it. I steal an occasional glance at the driver in the lane beside me. Can they hear it? Can they see my car shaking in its shocks? Or do they simply see a silly middle-aged woman slapping the steering wheel in time to music they can't hear?

Mid-life can make you do things totally out of character. A few years ago I put on dangling earrings for the first time. I immediately felt ten years younger. Arriving at a casual-dress summer meeting in leggings and an oversized bejeweled T-shirt, plus my earrings, I happily announced to my astounded (middle-aged) friends, "I'm having a mid-life breakout!"

I'm now addicted to dangling earrings.

If the mold you have poured yourself into over the years no longer fits, smash it. Or at least ease yourself out of it.

Realizing you don't fit the old mold—or have to—can be scary. It can also scare your spouse or anyone else who has assumed you would never change. Discovering who you are NOW, and where you want to go from here, is an essential element of successfully moving through the reluctant passage and arriving whole on the other side.

To do this, you need wisdom.

But where can you find the wisdom you need or know what path to take so that you ultimately accomplish God's purposes for you? Proverbs says a reverent relationship with the Lord is where we find knowledge for life.[2] Ask God to show you who you are now, muse over His shaping of your life, and pray over His plans for your future. As you do, answers will begin to take shape. The result can be a glimpse of exciting new horizons.

Ready for New Horizons

Seeker Questions

In contrast to the two-year-old inside who questions with strident tones and demands to know WHY, seeker questions float soft and deep, pensively searching for down-to-earth, definitive answers.

> What brings me a sense of accomplishment and satisfaction?
>
> Where do my spiritual gifts and natural talents lie?
>
> How has God shaped me through life's experiences?
>
> How have those experiences equipped me for the future?
>
> What stimulates me, moves me to tears, stirs me to passion?

Seeker questions bring out answers previously hidden from view. In time, these form the outline of a new life map.

A New Life Map

As an experienced kindergarten teacher, tutor, and workshop presenter on childhood issues, Karen planned to earn her master's degree in special education. "My goal had been shaped over several years," she recalls. "I was in charge of a special Sunday school class at my church for disabled children and saw how much the parents were helped by this ministry."

The mid-life passage, however, brought its own set of stress factors. Instead of going to graduate school, Karen found herself hospitalized for severe depression. Long repressed anguish from an abusive childhood savaged her sanity and left her suicidal.

Telling about the effect this had on her, she said, "After my breakdown, I was helped enormously by a Christian therapist. That experience made me evaluate my previous goals and radically change my direction in life. As I prayed for guidance, God led me to reconsider my previous goals and be open to a new life map. I still plan on going to graduate school, but now my passion is to become a family counselor and work with children and their parents."

Carol, a vivacious, snowy-haired seventy-year-old, also found new direction in mid-life. When I asked about her training as a marriage counselor she said, "I didn't begin college until I was fifty-five years old."

"Why did you wait so long?" I asked, surprised.

"Because I didn't think I could do the math at my age," she replied. "Then one day I thought, *How do I know if I never try? Maybe God has given me more ability than I've recognized so far.* So I went to college and to my delight got through the math. I realized it's never too late to do what you want to do, so I pushed on to get my master's degree, beginning my counseling practice at sixty-two."

Shedding Stereotypes

Ken Dychtwald, president of Age Wave, a company that serves the needs of the aging population, says of mid-life: "It's the most powerful and glorious segment of a person's life."[3] Coming to terms with the end of youth releases you to take a fresh look at the possibilities ahead.

In a poll of their readers, *Good Housekeeping* magazine discovered that women over forty were consistently the most admired.[4] Women who are seasoned politicians, diplomats, executives, high-ranking military officers, scientists, university professors, and rulers of countries or commerce are invariably in mid-life or older.

Rachel Carson completed *Silent Spring* at the age of fifty-five. When Margot Fonteyn danced as Juliet with Rudolf Nureyev, she was forty-seven and he was twenty-eight.

Britain's Emily Pankhurst started lobbying for women to have the vote when she was forty-five. Fifteen years later she celebrated its passing into law.[5]

Women in the second half of life have influenced every aspect of our lives. Margaret Thatcher swayed minds, Mother Teresa inspired hearts, and Erma Bombeck lightened daily life with humor.

It is a mistake to believe that life is a steady descent into uselessness once you're "over the hill"—unless you choose to waste the most powerful and glorious years available to you.

Stereotypes are self-imposed cages. The sooner you discard them and allow yourself freedom to dream, the better off you will be. If there was nothing to hinder you, what would you do? What would you like to do?

get additional schooling

find a more challenging job

learn a new language

picket in a protest

stretch yourself in a new ministry

In today's society, no woman is too old to go after her dreams or to get involved in issues that matter deeply to her.

Used wisely, mid-life can be your launching pad for personal and spiritual expansion.

Personal and Spiritual Expansion

After leaving a hectic yet intensely satisfying teaching ministry, I found myself free to do something else that mattered a great deal to me—helping women in trouble. Even though I had no personal exposure to domestic violence, as soon as I saw an appeal for volunteers to help in a women's shelter, I knew it was something I wanted to do.

At first, I answered phones and helped in whatever way I could. Later, because of my background in leading small groups, I was asked to facilitate a support group for the women. Reading stacks of books on the issues involved in domestic violence and hearing one woman after another share her story of abuse left me shaken.

Stepping into this foreign world forced me to grow. I heard language I'd never heard before. I found myself drawn to broken-hearted prostitutes and drug addicts who longed to be loved and cherished by someone.

Shattering the still-present myth that Christian men never batter their wives, a trembling sister-believer told me of her husband's repeated threats to kill her. Numb with outrage, I could only wrap my arms around her as she described his abusive behavior.

In that shelter for women wounded in body and spirit, God's love for a lost world and for me took on new meaning. Confronted by these women and the devastation sin had brought into their lives, the wonder and comfort of Christ offering himself up as a sacrifice for sin stirred me anew. As I drove to and from the shelter each week, my private chariot no longer reverberated to pulsating music. My car now became a meeting place with God, a private sanctuary where my emotions found release through prayer and worship.

When Jesus said, "I have come that they may have life, and have it to the full,"[6] He gave us the power to live life to the fullest no matter what age we are. God's purposes and plans are not stamped "past expiration date" once you cross into the second half of life. Instead, He urges you to use your talents, expand your horizons, plunge into opportunities to grow, and break through fears and stereotypes that hold you back.

To do that, let's begin to explore together some of the challenges we face in our muddled middle years.

2

Everything Seems
to Be Changing

"Guess what?" I said cheerfully to my college-age daughter. "I'm going to enroll in Bible school next semester."

Malaika's face registered the appropriate surprise, but I wasn't prepared for what came next. Like someone whose worst nightmare had come true, she cried, "Oh no, Mother— you're not going to be one of those *adult learners*, are you? We have them in our classes. They all sit up front and wave their hands to answer every question. They ruin the grading curve for the rest of us."

Despite her protest, I marched off to the registrar's office determined to stretch my gray matter around theology, philosophy, and the deeper meaning of life. I was also sure that no one would notice I was the age of their mother and a dreaded adult learner.

On the first day, in the first gathering of all the incoming students, a pimply-faced youth leaned toward me and asked, "Are you the instructor?"

Shocked, I muttered, "No." I wondered how he could tell I wasn't one of them.

When the real instructor strode in and handed out the intelligence tests, the other students confidently tackled question after question. I worked with equal gusto until I got to a sheet with strange diagrams all over it. No matter how I turned that paper around, I had no clue how to answer the questions under the diagrams. Time ran out. Flushed with embarrassment, I handed in all my papers.

My young friend turned to me once again. Smiling, he asked, "Was that tough for you?"

Despite my inability to analyze diagrams, they allowed me to enroll. In time, I recovered my shaken self-confidence. However, I quickly realized that my suits and heels just wouldn't do. I needed to blend in. After studying what the other female students were wearing, I decided to hit the junior department in a local dress shop. As I tried on skirts that stopped at my fingertips, eyed skinny little tops, and wondered about trendy, lace-up boots, my better judgment took control. Speaking in commanding tones to the juvenile within me, my inner parent scolded, "For goodness sake, get a grip. You can't wear those things, you are a middle-aged woman!" Fortunately, I listened.

Other priorities brought an end to my short-lived escapade as a forty-something college student, but not before I aced my classes. Crowing over my grades proved too much for my two children. Malaika, a college senior, and Elliot, a college freshman, gleefully pointed out that I had taken only six credit hours. If I had taken a full load the results might have been quite different. Perhaps.

Going back to college was like overdosing on Geritol. Brimming with energy, my mind worked overtime and every assignment became a personal challenge. Adding classes to my other commitments, however, made my comfortable journey through life accelerate into a heart-pumping power walk.

Jumping out of my easy routine dropped me directly into one of mid-life's most common experiences: a time of transition, stress, and growth. Whether stimulating, stretching, or scary—or all three at once—transition produces stress to one degree or another. Ideally, it also produces growth. When responded to wisely, I found that transitions yield many benefits: discovery of new abilities, expansion of horizons, deeper understanding of yourself, and greater awareness of God's presence in your life.

Going back to school brought me face-to-face with:

Transitions: changing roles, taking risks, exploring a new lifestyle.

Stress Factors: unfamiliar environments, fear of the unknown, fear of failure, multiple demands.

Resultant Growth: discovering abilities, experiencing success, exploring fresh paths, invigoration, challenge.

Sound familiar? Maybe your life is more like Katie's.

Katie's Story

Married to a highly successful yet frequently absent business-man, Katie's life centered on their two beautiful college-age daughters, Jill and Annette. Katie appeared to have every-thing a woman could want, yet she became deeply depressed, barely able to get out of bed each morning. Katie confided, "I had no idea what was wrong with me, but after struggling to function for three months, I knew I needed help."

Meeting weekly with a Christian counselor opened Katie's eyes to the role her upbringing and high expectations had in causing her depression. Then, before she could recover her own emotional stability, her previously predictable world slid into a five-year nightmare of one family crisis after another. Her oldest daughter, Jill, quit college after one semester and came home displaying all-too-familiar symptoms of depres-sion. Her father-in-law died of liver cancer, and her mother-in-law, also terminally ill, lived only two more years. A few months later, Annette, Katie's youngest daughter, came home from college struggling with anorexia. Dismayed, Katie told Annette, "You need help; I'll find you some." Then, on top of everything else, Jill announced she was pregnant.

Strengthened by discovering that her worth came from God's unconditional love, not from perfection, Katie reached out to her daughters with love, sensitively supporting them through many difficult months.

Today, nearly three years later, Jill and the father of her little girl are happily married. Annette, recovered from anorexia, went on to graduate from college and marry.

Because of the repeated upheavals of family crises, Katie experienced:

Transitions: involuntary family changes, loss of loved ones, removal of emotionally protective masks, upheavals in relationships.

Stress Factors: children struggling with adult development, terminal illnesses, inner drive for perfection, emotional demands from self and others that outstripped her resources.

In time, she emerged with:

Resultant Growth: self-understanding, striving for honesty, seeking fresh purpose and direction, accepting God's unconditional love.

Maybe you see yourself here.

Helen's Story

Helen had been widowed in her thirties with two sons to raise. Having successfully launched them into adulthood, she now found herself in her early fifties, still slender, attractive—and single.

After ten years in a job crackling with stress, Helen deserved her reputation as a top-notch legal assistant. When dealing with difficult clients, answering nonstop telephone calls, or handling reams of repetitive material she excelled, but Helen's sense of competence and safety relied on controlling her environment. When asked to be flexible, do unfamiliar tasks, or accept a redistribution of responsibilities, she balked. She also refused to cooperate with co-workers, leading to tensions within the office.

In addition to the emotional strain she experienced every day at work, Helen battled resentment at two other sources of stress—being unhappily single and having serious health problems.

Looking around at her friends—all moving through mid-life with a spouse alongside—she felt the pain of being alone. Why couldn't she have a husband, a cherished companion to grow old with? After years of focusing on the needs of her children, she pined for a marriage partner, but each year her hopes faded a little more. Helen's fears and frustrations were heightened by a bout with breast cancer that ultimately led to radical surgery.

Under the onslaught of these stressors, Helen became increasingly touchy and irritable at work. Finally, after several years of resisting changes in her workplace, she was given two choices: cooperate or leave.

She chose to leave.

"I was forced to look honestly at my response to what God allowed in my life," Helen acknowledged later. "I hadn't handled my circumstances well. I knew I couldn't change my marital status. However, I could do something about my resentful attitude.

"I started memorizing God's promises," she said excitedly. "Whenever I catch myself being negative about my circumstances, I remind myself of God's attitude toward me. Now that I'm learning to guard my mind against the lies I've told myself for so long, I feel quite differently about life."

Today, Helen not only has a satisfying job, she also enjoys new activities, friends, and a sense of fulfillment. She moved from barely surviving to thriving in the muddled middle years by a new understanding of:

Transitions: empty nest, health problems, financial concerns, job changes.

Stress Factors: releasing adult children, singleness, life-threatening illness, conflict in the workplace, loss of income.

Resultant Growth: greater dependence on God, honesty in failure, courage to identify personal needs, willingness to change responses to life.

Does your story in any way resemble Helen's?

Transitions Are a Normal Part of Life

In our forties and fifties, our perception of ourselves and how much time we have left begins to change. In and of itself midlife is a major life transition. Moreover, few of us navigate this passage without encountering a mix of other transitions.

So exactly what is a transition? What happens when we go through it? Are there recognizable stages? Can we identify some common feelings? Is it possible to anticipate what lies ahead?

Yes, Yes, Yes!

We've all seen children grow from helpless babies into "let me do it" toddlers. Clinging preschoolers grow into giggly first-graders, gawky junior-highers into high-school graduates, and college freshmen emerge as seniors ready to tackle the world. Life progresses, the child grows, finds a job, carves out a career, marries and has a family, or remains single. By the time we get to mid-life, we have lived through multiple cycles of physical and developmental changes.

I'm glad my days as a dependent child, an insecure teenager, or a naive twenty-year-old are over. I've become a woman with decades of life experience, wisdom, and perspective. It's stimulating to realize that more growth and development lie ahead.

Transitions Are an Inward Journey

The mid-life transition thrusts us out of the familiar. We lose our settled routines, defined roles, previous perceptions of ourselves, and goals and values we took for granted. Venturing into the unfamiliar, we move from who we were to who we are becoming.

Other circumstances coax or push us out of the comfortable into transition. Some transitions begin in response to a clear call from God. Others engulf us with no warning, leaving us shell-shocked and catapulted into changes we never anticipated. More commonly, we become aware of an impending transition through quiet, inner whisperings. These nudges of the heart point to unresolved pain, unmet needs, or a restlessness that cannot be stilled.

Transitions Are Times of Opportunity

Transitions are a normal part of life and an inward journey. W. Bridges, author of *Transitions*,[1] describes them also as times of opportunity. Approached wisely, they become stopping-off places, platforms from which to take in the sweep of where we have been, who we are now, and where we want to go. A transition is a time to retool, rediscover, and redefine who you are.

Difficult choices are often part of this process. The Bible illustrates this in the Old Testament story of Ruth. Widowed as a young woman, Ruth faced serious choices. Should she go back to her own Moabite family? Try to persuade Naomi, her Israelite mother-in-law, to stay in Moab? Or should she go with Naomi to Israel, turning her back on her own family, culture, and land?

Weighing all sides of such a life-changing decision, Ruth refused to sever the loving bonds that intertwined her life with Naomi's. She pled with her mother-in-law, "Don't urge me to leave you or to turn back from you. Where you go I will go, and where you stay I will stay. Your people will be my people and your God my God. Where you die I will die, and there I will be buried."[2] Ruth chose to say goodbye to all she had known. This time of transition became an opportunity for retooling, rediscovering, and redefining who she was. In the process, she discovered what she believed and the core values that guided her life.

Stages of Transition

Any transition process is marked by three stages. Being aware of these stages and the emotions that accompany them help us make sense of what is happening. We'll call these three stages *farewell, fallow time,* and *fresh beginnings.*

Initial Stage: Farewell

In describing the stages of transition, Bridges pictures them as seasons of the year. The first stage is like fall. In that season of cascading leaves—in hues of fiery red, mustard, orange, and chestnut—the silent message is heard: *Change is coming.* The leaves, once green heralds of a coming season of beauty and vitality, are now dry and crackling underfoot.

Farewells signal endings to the familiar. Sometimes farewells are preceded by boredom and restlessness. Other times we're plunged into change and farewells without warning. Katie, the mother of two grown daughters, experienced this. She found herself an unwilling participant on an emotional roller coaster. When would the chaos end? When would her dreams for her daughters finally come true? Whether arising from within or without, farewells embody some of the following:

saying goodbye to former routines and relationships;

letting go of old roles and priorities that once defined you;

acknowledging and releasing aspects of life that no longer reflect who you are and the direction your life has taken;

shedding self-perceptions that hinder growth; and

experiencing feelings of grief or joy, mourning or celebration, loss or gain.

When something precious comes to an end it's painful to let go, but that's what you have to do if there is to be a fresh beginning. This also applies to saying farewell to the young woman you once were. Releasing yourself from the myth of being forever youthful is one of the more difficult, yet essential, aspects of mid-life. The result, ultimately, is being free to value and accept yourself on a deeper level. Before you reach the joy of a fresh beginning, however, there is a middle stage to journey through.

Middle Stage: Fallow Time

Just as fall represents transition's first stage, farewells, so the seeming deadness of the winter landscape reflects the emotions of the second stage, fallow time. Helen, struggling to get over the shock of leaving her job under unpleasant circumstances, quickly found herself engulfed by feelings of:

> confusion, emotional detachment, dislocation, a state of suspension;
>
> distress, accompanied by a painful sense of loneliness and separation;
>
> loss of purpose and direction; and
>
> fear that life might never be fulfilling again.

These are difficult emotions to deal with. If your children have moved out of the nest, or some significant role has come to an end, it's normal to wonder if your life will ever have purpose again.

"I felt so uncomfortable grappling with these feelings of transition," Helen confessed ruefully, "that I moved too quickly and unwisely. I thought the solution to my pain was to rush out and find a better job. After all, I wouldn't feel like a failure if I could do that."

Shaking her head, she acknowledged, "I didn't give myself time to evaluate what had gone wrong or where I needed to implement changes before jumping into my next job. I lasted only one week."

Instead of trying to erase the painful emotions of fallow time and possibly living to regret it, it is wiser to pray, slow down, and look to God to direct your path. Now is the time to reflect, think, evaluate, learn, and wait. He knows what you are going through.

Underneath the emotional dreariness that often marks fallow time, renewal is astir. Keep waiting. Hold on. Even though you don't see it now, at the right moment springlike shoots of hope will make their appearance, signaling the beginning of transition's final stage—fresh beginnings.

Final Stage: Fresh Beginnings

Katie realized that God really *did* care about what was happening in her life and in her personally. When she took time out to talk with God, something amazing happened.

"As my energy and enthusiasm for life returned," Katie said with a warm smile, "I determined to go back to college and finish my degree. After having put aside for twenty-five years my goal of graduating, I'm determined to see it through."

In working through her painful transition, Helen learned through prayer some surprising truths about her own inner needs. Reflecting on her experience of growth, she commented, "God helped me realize I needed people and that I could bring joy into my own life by looking outside myself and caring about others."

Both Katie and Helen welcomed their fresh beginnings. They also discovered energy and hope welling up from within, giving new meaning to what they had gone through.

These signs signal the third stage of transition:

renewed confidence in God's plans for your good;

fresh bursts of energy, ideas, and desires;

Holy Spirit boldness to attempt something new;

confidence, joy, a sense of challenge;

creativity, a desire to explore and expand your horizons; and

a thankful attitude.

Stress Factors

I found being a baby-boomer student to be both stimulating and challenging. But I was under pressure and demanded more of myself physically, mentally, and emotionally.

In response to those demands, our bodies release adrenaline into the bloodstream, preparing us for "fight or flight." Too little stress and we feel understimulated, bored, maybe even depressed. Too much or too frequent stress causes the outpouring of adrenaline to produce symptoms ranging in severity from headaches to heart trouble. Protecting ourselves from chronic stress as we go through mid-life is vital for long-term health.

The answer isn't to avoid growing through new challenges, but rather discovering how to manage the stress that accompanies growth.

A good place to start is by responding to Jesus' invitation: "Come to me all you who are weary and burdened, and I will give you rest." The apostle Peter counsels, "Commit [yourself] to [your] faithful Creator."[3] Many centuries earlier, the prophet Isaiah had also promised perfect peace to those who fix their minds on God.[4] For the most concentrated dose of powerful anti-stress advice, digest the Psalms on a daily basis. Skewed perspectives or misplaced priorities are easier to identify and change when you remember that God is your refuge, defender, and source of strength.

In addition to prayer and reliance on God, here are some other ways to reduce pressure on yourself:

Slow your pace in life.

Realize saying "yes" means saying "no" to something else.

Search out solutions to long-term, unresolved issues.

Lower your expectations of yourself and others.

Eat wisely, get more sleep, and exercise.[5]

By taking control of your life with these and other healthy responses to stress, you'll be free to grow into the person God designed you to be.

Resultant Growth

Throughout the Bible, God makes clear that He actively seeks our good and our growth. He works all things together for our ultimate good, sees our potential, and gives us abilities He wants us to use.[6] God's desired outcome for any transition, whether sought out by us or brought into our lives by unexpected circumstances, is always personal and spiritual growth.

Growth Comes Through Risk-Taking

"Nothing ventured, nothing gained." Whenever you do something you have never done before, you are taking a risk. For most of us, this brings uncomfortable feelings and a degree of anxiety. Add these feelings to an active imagination and you get sweaty palms, a thumping heart, a dry mouth, and an absolute determination not to attempt something you're sure is beyond you. But refuse to risk and attempt the new, and life shrinks into a shadow of what it could be.

Growth requires that we go beyond familiar boundaries and push ourselves toward what seems out of reach. To do this we must:

> consciously trust God to supply our needs as we step into opportunities He brings.[7]
>
> rely on the truth that God is at work in us to will and to act according to His good purpose.[8]
>
> take whatever steps are needed to live a more fulfilling and Christ-honoring life.[9]

Growth Comes Through Persevering

Growth invariably means persevering through feelings that scream *no* and circumstances that don't change. We wish we didn't have to wait for events to take their course or for God to answer our prayers.

However, through the process of persevering we discover inner strengths, develop new skills, and overcome daunting obstacles. And there are even rewards for this—a positive sense of accomplishment and success, increased confidence to face what comes next, and a deeper faith.

Growth Comes Through Right Choices

Life doesn't just happen to us: our growth is directly linked to the choices we make. Katie learned this when she chose not to hide her depression or deny the pain she saw in her daughters' lives. Instead, she actively chose paths that led to healing for each of them.

You have the power to choose your responses to life's surprises. You decide whether you are victim or victor—whether to rage, rebel, or rest in God. You choose whether to say yes or no to what lies before you. God has given you the ability and the responsibility to gather information, consult Scripture, evaluate options, solicit opinions, and make decisions—even change your mind. All these processes produce growth.

Ultimately, you choose whether to accept difficult situations and grow by them, wallow in denial, or wrap yourself in self-pity. Your choices, to a great extent, determine the future direction of your life.

Growth Comes Through Personal Change

Growth also comes when you have the courage to evaluate your actions and attitudes and make necessary changes. When Helen honestly faced who she had become, her heartfelt response was, "Oh, God, please show me how to change." With his help, she actively sought ways to nurture herself spiritually, emotionally, and physically.

Most of us have struggled to change our negative attitudes or alter behavior patterns that create conflict. We know it's not easy, but with God's Word to guide us and his Spirit to empower us, we can be different. In the mid-life transition, we *can* become more like Christ.

Now that we know how change affects our lives, we're ready to explore more issues facing us in these middle years. We'll tackle the hardest subject first: Who is that woman in the mirror?

3

Who *Is* That in the Mirror?

I knew I was in for a hard time when I discovered my first gray hairs at the age of thirty. Horrified, I thought, *This is awful. I'm too young to have gray hair*. But suddenly I knew what I would do. I'd always wanted to be a blonde, so I headed to the store for hair color. In one stroke I would both realize my secret dream of being a blonde *plus* hide those few gray hairs.

Rushing home, magic shampoo in hand, I wasted no time in becoming the new me. Six weeks later, my husband and I went on a holiday. Walking through an airport on our trip home, Jim ran into a colleague of his. I paused and glanced in a mirror. Aghast, I stared at a dark, one-inch grow-out.

The next day I went to a hairdresser. I pleaded, "Please put me back to my natural color. I don't want to keep on dying my hair." The only problem is that natural dark hair has subtle shading, and dyed dark hair looks like a solid black helmet permanently attached to your head—at least mine did. Slinking out of the salon, I vowed no friend would see me in public wearing my black helmet!

So back at the drugstore, I discovered another bottle of magic—a color stripper. The results it promised seemed to be written with me in mind. To be safe, I bought another shampoo-in hair color in a more natural-looking shade. When the stripper took effect, I had yet another hair color: orange! Terrified, I hurriedly shampooed in the new color, praying it would take. Actually, it wasn't too bad.

Two weeks later, I decided it would be fun to get a curly perm. Clipping a coupon for an unknown beauty shop, I made an appointment. There wasn't a soul in sight when I walked in. That should have told me something. I've since learned—never frequent an empty beauty shop!

I quickly explained to the hairdresser what had happened to my hair: "I colored my hair, then stripped the color out, and then colored it again. Are you sure it will be okay if it's permed?"

"Oh, no problem," she replied, "there's nothing to worry about."

She sat me down, gave me my perm, then disappeared to talk on the telephone for what seemed like forever. I kept hoping she knew what she was doing. She eventually returned, washed out the solution, and then tried to style it. I heard her mutter, "A little conditioner will help this." Looking in the mirror, I gasped. My hair stuck out from my head like steel wool.

Desperate, I went back to the hairdresser who had given me the black helmet and begged her to trim my hair into some sort of shape. I walked out of there with hair an inch long all over.

Knowing Jim doesn't like short hair, I guessed what his reaction would be. I wasn't surprised.

The next day I bought a wig. It was sleek and sophisticated, and people complimented me on my new hairdo wherever I went. I decided to wear it forever.

A few months later, I went to collect my three-year-old son, Elliot, from a friend who was taking care of him. She was one of those women who never has a hair out of place, who doesn't know what a split nail is. I scooped up my son, and while my friend and I chatted, Elliot reached for my hair. In one brisk tug he had the wig in his hand. Needless to say, I was mortified. It was the last time I wore a wig.

Today, twenty years later, it isn't gray hair that gets my attention. (That gets taken care of by a beautician who knows what she's doing.) Now I stare at my face in the mirror and ask, *Who is that person?*

If we know we are more than our physical appearance, why do we place so much value on looking young and attractive? Should we really be doing all we can to hide the inevitable, or should we accept aging without a fight? I wanted some sane, biblical answers.

In Bondage to Youth and Beauty

I invited six friends over one evening for a frank discussion about mid-life. We were a diverse group. Some worked full time, some part time, some were homemakers involved in church, school, or community activities. A couple of them had been through menopause and took hormone replacement therapy. A few exercised regularly, others not at all. But with our ages spanning the early forties to the late fifties, we shared one thing in common: we were in mid-life.

For a while, we all talked at once—seven women trying to catch up on one another's lives. Then I announced the reason for our gathering: "Let's talk about mid-life and how we are affected by it."

I asked the first question: "Why is staying young and beautiful so important in our culture?"

Janet, an office manager, spoke up: "I think it's because we are surrounded by messages from the cosmetic industry: aging is bad; looking older is a negative. They say, use our products and get rid of unsightly wrinkles; use our revolutionary cream and turn back the clock. Whether it's Clinique or Estée Lauder or Revlon, we're bombarded with negative messages and false promises."

"I have to confess," rejoined Elaine, "I'm always looking for a 'fountain of youth' somewhere. I prowl the cosmetic aisles and natural food stores hoping to find *something* that will stop the wrinkles and cure the fat."

She looked around at the others. "Unless you live in another world, the pressure to be thin, have the perfect hairdo, look gorgeous, and be sharply dressed is hard to resist. What are we supposed to do?"

Laughing, I said, "You could have plastic surgery. I heard a doctor describe the ideal surgically renovated face. The surgeon claimed assertive, athletic eyelids are in. As well as fuller, richer lips, high cheekbones, and a stronger chin."

Everyone groaned.

"And if there's room on your credit card, you can slip into your doctor's office in the morning for a few 'nips and tucks' and be home by dinnertime. Don't plan on going back to work the next day, though."

Because our culture places such a high value on what is only skin-deep, men and women live in fear of losing their youthful looks. As women are increasingly emancipated from strictly defined roles and horizons, we now find ourselves in danger of being chained again—to youthfulness at all costs. (And it *does* cost.) From hours in a health club—stair-stepping and sculpting our bodies by pumping iron—to megabucks at the beauty counter buying the latest revolutionary discovery, staying "young" is expensive. We might be able to retard the visible evidence of getting older, but we cannot stop the clock.

I told my six friends about an acquaintance in her late thirties who had applied for a job as a sportswear designer. "She told me that even though she is a Christian, she felt she had no choice but to lie about her age. She was convinced she wouldn't have had a chance at getting the job if she'd told the truth."

Bondage Begins at Birth

Jane, a new grandmother, spoke next. "I think the pressure to be beautiful begins at birth. Even though I know I would love my new granddaughter no matter how she looked, for some reason it's important to me that she is a pretty baby."

"I know what you mean," I said. "I remember how I felt as a new mother showing off my firstborn to family and friends. I waited to hear words of praise and admiration, but I never stopped to ask myself why it mattered so much. Now I think I've figured it out. I was looking for affirmation of my worth and my baby's in their 'oohs' and 'aahs.'"

Like all moms, I needed others to tell me I had produced an attractive child. If no one said, "Oh, what an adorable baby!" or, "She is so pretty," rightly or wrongly, I would have been crushed and embarrassed. Without realizing it at the time, my worth and my baby's were dependent on the response of others to her appearance.

"It's so unfair when you think about it," said Janet, "that worth and beauty are linked. It usually *is* the cutest toddlers or the perkiest grade-schoolers who get the attention."

"I can remember to this day," said Debbie, a petite blonde, "the pain I felt as an eight-year-old when a classmate called me a wart." Blinking back tears, she went on, "I asked him why he called me that, and he said because I was small and ugly. I've never forgotten his cruel remark. In fact, for most of my life I thought he was right."

Molded by the Media

"Oh, Debbie, that must have been so painful for you," I consoled. "Children are particularly sensitive to remarks like that. But why do you think grown women struggle with how they look?"

"That's easy," Janet chimed in, her voice rising. "Turn on the TV or flip through a magazine. Young, attractive women advertise everything from cars to silky underwear. If your eyelids droop or you have a few lines on your face, you feel like it's all over."

Elaine noted, "Older women in commercials are selling Fixadent or Depends. They've got us convinced those ailments are just around the corner."

Margaret, a multitalented businesswoman, spoke quietly. "We need to analyze how the media portrays older women and weigh it against reality. Think of the women you know who are ten or twenty years older. Aging affects each of them differently. There are no stereotypes."

Agreeing with Margaret, we decided our minds are too easily influenced by the media. The glamorizing of youth and beauty and the negative portrayals of older women do affect us. Unless we're aware of the distortions that are shaping our attitudes, we will continue to revere youth and be repulsed by signs of aging.

Beauty Has Its Rewards

"What does beauty do for a woman?" I asked.

Janet jumped right in. "It gives her power," she said emphatically. "If you're beautiful, all you have to do is bat your eyelashes and men fall all over themselves to please you—socially and in the workplace."

"It gives her opportunities for advancement," Elaine added. "You may be a bimbo, but if you have the right face and body, doors open up. Take a look at *People* magazine. Check out the photos on the society page of the newspaper. Watch the Emmys or the Oscars. You don't see your average 'Plain Jane' hanging on the arm of the rich and famous."

"Unfortunately, you're right," agreed Kathleen. "Women are rewarded for being young and beautiful. Men, money, fame, popularity, and power—all the 'good things' in life—come more easily to great-looking women."

The Fear of Aging

After discussing what women gain from beauty, I posed another question. "What's behind our fear of getting older?"

Continuing her thought that women lose their sense of worth as they get older, Janet shared, "I feel like I'm invisible now that I'm in mid-life. I must admit I enjoyed the admiring glances I got when I was younger. Now people, men in particular, walk past me like I don't exist."

"I can relate," Elaine agreed. "I've accepted that men don't look at me like they used to, but now I struggle with being called 'Grandma!' I hate the title. I've told my grandson to call me 'Nana.' I feel I'm too young to fit the stereotype of a little old woman with sensible shoes and her hair in a bun."

Margaret chuckled. "You certainly don't fit the stereotype of a grandma," she said. "But there are different ways of looking at our predicament. A woman can be fifty and *act* like seventy. Physically, two women can be exactly the same age—but one may run a marathon while the other can hardly make it to the mailbox."

Elaine nodded. "Socially, a mid-life mom with small children seems younger than someone like me, who has grandchildren. The greatest factor, though, is psychological. How old do you *feel?* If you feel old, you'll act old, and if you feel young, you'll live accordingly. You'll enjoy life. The choice is ours."

So how we feel and how we view ourselves determines our response to this stage of our lives. Some women fear the passing of years. They fear prejudice in the marketplace, physical infirmity, loss of mental quickness. And those who derive their sense of worth from their appearance will most certainly struggle.

"I like to look as attractive as I can," Kathleen admitted, "but I refuse to base my self-worth on how I *look*. I want to be emotionally healthy as I get older, not embarrassed about my appearance. Knowing God accepts me as I am helps me to see myself as a valuable human being. I hope because I've grown a little wiser through the years, I'll have more to give to others."

Finding the Balance

Kathleen's perceptive comments moved our discussion in a new direction. "If our worth doesn't come from our appearance," I suggested, "should we just let it all hang out? Does escaping the bondage of youth and beauty mean we throw out salads and self-restraint and indulge in chocolate and wear elastic waistbands?"

We laughed, passed the cookies, and launched into the next round of conversation: finding the balance.

Fearfully and Wonderfully Made

"As a Christian," Janet said, "I view my body as belonging to the Lord. So, no, I don't think we should let it all hang out. We don't have to be fanatical about our appearance, but taking care of the one body God has given us seems like the right thing to do. There are, of course, a lot of changes with the onset of menopause, and we need to be aware of those and what we can do about it."

"I agree," said Debbie. "The word of God teaches that we are fearfully and wonderfully made and that our bodies are the temple of the Holy Spirit. I believe I honor the Lord when I take care of myself.[1] I try to walk every day, and I take a calcium supplement. I know some women actually get shorter after menopause, and I'm only four-eleven now!"

"Although estrogen may not be the answer for everyone," Margaret added, "I've found hormone supplements have helped me a great deal."

In their book *Menopause and Mid-Life*,[2] Dr. Robert and Mary Wells describe the various symptoms of menopause and tell us that osteoporosis can be a major problem for women in this category. According to Dr. Wells, women can lose up to 30 percent of their skeletal mass in their fifties and sixties. The majority of this bone loss occurs in the first five years after menopause, making it vital that younger women guard against this by taking sufficient calcium.

Recognizing the symptoms of menopause leads to better physical and emotional health in mid-life. Some women encounter symptoms years earlier, but the average age for menopause is fifty-one. In his book, Dr. Wells lists the following common indicators of menopause:

Menstrual irregularity: hormonal changes affect the length of the monthly cycle. Different bleeding patterns occur, including possible mid-cycle bleeding.

Hot flashes and night sweats: these can occur five to ten years before the last period. Up to 80 percent of menopausal women experience hot flashes ranging from brief feelings of warmth to several minutes of heat and drenching sweat.

Sleep disturbances: insomnia is considered an early sign of menopause brought on by low estrogen levels. Hot flashes also contribute to sleep disturbances, resulting in general fatigue and emotional stress.

Feeling tired all the time: one of the most common symptoms is lacking the energy to keep up a normal pace.

Emotional swings: depression, irritability, crying for no reason, memory loss.

Joint pain: a number of women experience pain in their joints even though test results are normal.

Vaginal changes: these tend to occur after the other symptoms appear and become progressively worse unless treated. Without treatment, these changes can lead to shrinkage of vaginal tissue and pain during sexual intercourse.

Anyone who experiences these symptoms should see her doctor for an estrogen test and decide together how to respond.

In addition to going through menopause during mid-life, we are also at greater risk for cancer, diabetes, and heart disease. Occurrence of breast cancer is now one in nine during a woman's lifetime, making self-examinations, mammograms, and a yearly checkup essential. To insure the best quality of life, exercise on a regular basis, monitor your food intake, and modify your schedule so that your body gets the rest and attention it needs.

Adjusting to Mid-Life

"Before we end our discussion," I said, "I'd like each of you to share some conclusive thoughts. First, how can we value ourselves and grow inwardly as we get older? And, second, is there some Scripture that has encouraged you or helped to shape your perspective?"

Adopt a Positive Attitude Toward Yourself

"I feel that thinking negatively about ourselves does more damage than the physical changes that occur," Elaine said convincingly. "Even though the apostle Paul may not have had women in mid-life in mind when he said, *Though outwardly we are wasting away, yet inwardly we are being renewed day by day*, it is a fact of life.[3] Because of our relationship with Jesus, we can have a positive attitude toward ourselves, and we can have the inner strength we need each day for whatever lies ahead."

Invest in Others

"If we fear growing older, we are fearing a new stage of life, and we miss its opportunities for growth," Debbie said. "The Psalms say we will still bear fruit in our old age and will stay fresh and green. God wants us to keep bearing fruit, reaching out to others, passing on what we've learned. And one more thing I've noticed: younger women want to have a relationship with older women. I find a great sense of fulfillment spending time on a regular basis with a few younger women. I think they value my input, and I enjoy passing on what I've learned about life and about the Lord."

Maintain Your Style

"We probably all know the verse in Proverbs 31 that speaks of our charm and beauty fading, but the woman who fears the Lord will be praised,"[4] Kathleen said. "I agree with that, but looking attractive and well dressed does make a difference in our society. People seem to treat us differently when we're well dressed than when we're in our grubbies. Plus, I think looking our best gives us a sense of confidence."

As we nodded in agreement, Kathleen added, "There's a difference between finding your value in how you look and caring about your appearance because you value and respect yourself."

Glancing at my watch, I asked for quick comments from the rest.

Broaden Your Concept of Beauty

Margaret began, "Perhaps we need to redefine beauty to mean more than physical attractiveness. I see beauty in the lined faces of many older women who have had a deep relationship with the Lord. The truly beautiful woman has a glow—a softness and radiance that comes from within, whether or not she wears blush. My sense of value as a woman loved by God increases the more I seek the things that are above.[5] Growing older is something that happens to me beyond my control, but it doesn't have to affect how I view myself."

Nurture Yourself

"In mid-life, many of us are involved to one degree or another in caring for family members," Janet reminded us. "It's good and right for us to do this. But we can end up burned-out, depressed, or sick, particularly if we are holding down a job, running a home, and involved heavily at church, too. I know my energy level is not what it was twenty years ago. I'm convinced that if we don't nurture ourselves during these middle years, we'll pay the price sooner than is necessary."

Cultivate an Eternal Outlook

"The awareness of my mortality hit me full force when I saw my first grandchild," Jane said. "Part of the internal adjustment that we wrestle with is this very issue. I know that most people are uncomfortable talking about death, but the reality is our bodies are not going to live forever. I believe, of course, that if we put our faith in Christ we will live eternally with Him.[6] I think a lot about what heaven will be like. It will be more wonderful than anything I've known, and holding on to that thought helps me not to fear growing old. Right now, my goal is to enjoy life and to live each day aware of the Lord's presence with me. That's the key to everything."

Growing older is inevitable! But your view of it makes all the difference. It can be a nightmare to be avoided at all costs, or an adventure to be embraced. In mid-life, youth and beauty fade. But a new loveliness can emerge on a deeper level as you grow into a woman of faith, compassion, knowledge, humor, and life experience.

Now that we've broached the subject of growing old, let's examine the unique challenges of mid-life marriage: renewing and rekindling the ties that bind.

4

"Will You Still Love Me
When I'm . . . ?"

I set my suitcase on the floor of the hotel room and closed the door with a sigh of relief. The telephone startled me. *Who could be calling me . . . here in Melbourne, Australia?* I knew my husband, Jim, was coming from Sydney to meet me, but our eagerly anticipated rendezvous was still three days away.

Puzzled, I reached for the telephone. "Hi!" a familiar voice said. "How are you?"

"Jim!" I responded with surprise. "Where are you? I thought you were in the middle of the outback."

"I'm in the lobby," he said with a laugh. "We must have missed each other. I've been waiting for you to get here from the airport for over an hour. I'll come up right away."

Feeling like a girl about to see the date of her dreams, I rushed to the door. Waving excitedly from the second-floor balcony, I watched as my husband of twenty-seven years strode across the parking lot toward the stairway, looking, at least to me, like an American version of Crocodile Dundee.

In the four weeks I had been traveling and speaking to women all across Australia, we had seen each other once. We couldn't wait to be together again.

Mid-life marriage—shimmering with romance and bubbling with excitement. A perfect blend of independence and intimacy, affirmation and emotional satisfaction. Sounds like an advertisement for discount weddings at a Las Vegas chapel. But let's be honest. *Shimmering with romance* and *bubbling with excitement* don't always describe marriage in mid-life.

The bathroom door opened suddenly, making me jump. I thought Jim had already left for his usual twelve-hour day at the hospital.

"Tom forgot to pick me up," he said irritably. "You'll have to get out of the shower right away and take me to work." Unable to hear him clearly above the din of the water, I asked him to repeat what he'd said. His tone seethed with frustration and impatience.

Equally irritated, I shouted, "I can't! I'm shampooing my hair."

"You don't have to dry your hair or put makeup on to take me to the hospital! Just grab some clothes and let's go." Sensing that I was about to protest again, Jim said, "Oh forget it, I'll take my car and meet you back here at noon. Don't forget, you have to take me to the airport."

Five minutes past noon, Jim flung open the back door of our house. "Are you ready? Let's go. I'm driving *my* car to the airport because this trip is a business expense. You'll have to drive it home."

Frustration mixed with fear gripped me. "You know I'm not comfortable with a stick shift. Why can't we take my car?" By now the mood between us was icy.

Driving to the airport in *my* car, Jim asked, "Have you been keeping track of the mileage for your tax deductions?"

Taking a deep breath, I replied lightly, "No, I haven't. Quite honestly, I had totally forgotten about doing that for the last few months." Grim-faced, Jim stared straight ahead, and I wondered what else we could fight over.

After five minutes of silence, I asked, "Are you stressed out from work or are you mad at me?"

"Both," he replied. "I'm sorry for snapping at you, but on days like today, I need your cooperation."

For the rest of the trip we actually listened in turn to each other's frustrations, expectations, and need for understanding. By the time Jim had unloaded his bags curbside, the icy atmosphere between us had melted. Smiling, I gave him a hug. "Next time we get riled up," I said, "let's talk it out instead of taking it out on each other."

"Good idea," he said, leaning over to give me a quick but warm farewell kiss.

Mid-Life Marriage: Fulfillment or Frustration?

A marriage of many years can be a source of great emotional fulfillment . . . or it can be a source of great emotional frustration.

Mike and Linda bear out the findings of research that a satisfying long-term relationship enhances well-being.[1] Celebrating their twenty-fifth anniversary at a surprise party planned by their two daughters, the couple sparkled with happiness. In addition to their mutual attraction and acceptance of each other, what bound them together was their shared history of family, friends, and life experiences.

When asked how they had achieved their successful marriage, they looked at each other and smiled. Mike spoke first. "Success didn't come easily. It took determination and dependence on God to make it work. We are so different from each other. We've clashed over things like handling our finances, how tidy the house should be, and whether or not the dog should be allowed inside the house."

Linda added, "Having worked through all kinds of differences, I feel we've learned important lessons for the future. We feel very comfortable with each other and confident about our relationship. I pray that we'll continue to grow as a couple through whatever stresses mid-life brings."

Unfortunately, there are couples with marriages of fifteen, twenty, or thirty years who don't find themselves in such good shape. Their marriages are like empty husks.

Betty and Peter's thirty-year marriage bears no resemblance to their wedding-day dreams. Stagnation has set in, and the magical chemistry has vanished. Long-ago promises to love and cherish, though given sincerely, mock what their marriage has become.

Tears threatened to overflow as Betty described her marriage. "Peter has become a recluse. He goes to work and comes home, but he won't go to church anymore. All he wants to do is be by himself . . . with his computer. He won't talk, and he doesn't want to socialize . . . period. He doesn't even care what he looks like anymore."

Many couples find it too complex and painful to try to change the destructive patterns they have established over the years. One or both partners might want to cast off the mind-numbing monotony of daily life or break through walls of emotional indifference, but memories of deep hurts coupled with fear of more pain kill the spark needed to act. It becomes easier to survive by hiding from their emotions and putting on a guise of happiness. Believing nothing can change, they settle for less than God intended.

In mid-life, the marriage relationship needs special attention. After years of familiarity—and maybe neglect—it needs to be revisited, renewed, rekindled. Given this level of attention, love will not only survive but thrive in the years ahead.

Revisiting Your Marriage

I laughed in rueful recognition at the cartoon. "Ready for some excitement, honey?" a balding husband asks his wife as they sit in separate armchairs watching television. "Let's switch chairs!"

Established marriages need some excitement, and if switching chairs does the trick for you, do it . . . but don't stop there. Take the time to think seriously about your marriage, discovering its strengths and confronting its weaknesses. If you conduct a "mid-life checkup" you can pinpoint areas that need work now, before future stresses compound problems. To build a thriving relationship that will survive mid-life and beyond, you'll need to ask yourself a few probing questions.

Before you begin, though, stop and pray. Ask God to help you clear away negative attitudes, to forgive where necessary, and to come to a fresh understanding of and love for your imperfect spouse. Remember, you too are imperfect.

Without the Holy Spirit's presence, honestly examining your marriage could plunge you into anger, self-pity, or despair. With God's help, however, you can receive the comfort, insight, and strength-giving hope you need.

Kick off your marriage checkup on a positive note by asking yourself the following:

When I think of my husband, what makes my spirits soar?

What blessings has he brought into my life?

How has he influenced me for good?

After building your courage by thinking about some of the strengths of your marriage, give your frank response to the following:

What frustrates me most in our marriage?

How could our marriage bring us greater satisfaction?

What will our relationship look like in five or ten years if we make no changes?

Let's continue our candid look at the state of some mid-life marriages. Reality isn't always pleasant, but renewal and rekindling will only happen when we identify where change is needed. Take a deep breath, plunge in, and see if any of these images describe your relationship:

A Stagnant Pool. Nothing's happening. The lines of communication are down.

Evaluation Time: How would you rate your communication patterns? "We have communication problems," said a frustrated wife to her husband in a true-to-life cartoon. His response? "I told you we shouldn't have switched from AT&T." If you fear a similar reply, it's a clue you're on different wavelengths. Are you able to share feelings as well as facts and opinions? Do you talk through differences and bring resolution, even if you agree to disagree?

Ticket for One. Interdependence and intimacy is sacrificed on the altar of independence and pursuit of individual goals.

Evaluation Time: Is there a mutually satisfying balance between independent pursuits and togetherness? With no societal barriers to your dreams and ambitions, what priority does your husband's schedule, needs, and desires have? Do your activities nurture your relationship or cause you to neglect it?

A Hot Air Popcorn Popper. A little heat and the kernels fly in every direction.

Evaluation Time: Are fast and furious exchanges a frequent occurrence? Are words used to stab and wound, to manipulate, to win the war between the two of you? Is a soft answer and self-control rejected by either of you in favor of victory? If you are in an angry, emotionally destructive relationship, what are you doing about it?

A Family Museum. Kept open for the family to visit. Features artifacts and memories of long ago.

Evaluation Time: With the children gone, what remains between the two of you? What steps are necessary to rebuild the companionship you once shared? What interests do you now share and what new areas could you explore together? How important is laughter to you? Do you have deep mutual friendships that enrich your lives as a couple, or do you need to build this element into your relationship?

A Silent Contract. Unspoken agreements allow the playing out of unhealthy marital roles.

Evaluation Time: Who are you now that you've grown up? In her book *Second Honeymoon*,[2] marriage therapist Dr. Sonya Rhodes describes various roles husbands and wives assume. One is labeled "Daddy's Little Girl." In this relationship, a wife puts her husband in a father-substitute role, looking to him to give her personal worth, meaning, happiness, and fulfillment. In turn, the husband's emotional needs are met by having a dependent, little-girl-like wife. Could this describe you? Or do you see yourself as a whole and capable person, yet at the same time deeply loving and appreciating your spouse?

Another common silent contract is that of "Enabler/Receiver." This relationship takes nurturing beyond healthy boundaries. Are you always the giver, the sacrificer, the one who adjusts your schedule and priorities? Is this taken for granted? Or does your husband flex with your needs?

Could you be an "Eternal Mother," clinging to your adult children, insisting they come over often? Do your plans always include the children and grandchildren? How are you shifting your focus from your former identity as *mother* to include wife and individual? You will continue to be *mother*, but releasing that primary identity frees you to discover who else you are. Perhaps an exciting woman your husband has yet to meet?

After revisiting your relationship, you face critical decisions: Will you choose to take the easy way out and say goodbye? Will you grieve over what you see and sink into bitterness or apathy? Or, will you thank God for the man He has given you, warts and all, and renew your determination to keep your marriage fresh and growing by being willing, yourself, to change?

Renewing Your Commitment

"Bob's naturally pessimistic personality turned even more negative and critical soon after we moved to California," Carole confided. She wore a short, curly hairstyle, befitting her bouncy personality and quick smile. But she spoke bluntly of the difficulties in her marriage.

"One Christian counselor I talked to suggested I divorce Bob," she said, raising her eyebrows in mock shock. "I didn't see that as an option and decided to change counselors. I'm glad I did, because the next one helped us both."

Carole's husband had become sour and disruptive at work. After several warnings, he was offered a severance package and asked to leave. As months slipped by with no work he sank deeper and deeper into depression. With her strong faith in God and cheerful disposition, Carole managed to hold the family together during this time. But the crisis took its toll.

"After a long year, Bob finally took a job that paid half his former salary. With the little I make working part time in a supermarket, we are at least paying our bills," she added, shaking her head sadly.

"When we got married," Carole continued, "I assumed he would be the breadwinner and I would raise a houseful of kids. Now I feel married to one. It's not ideal, but if I were the emotionally sick one I'd hope he'd stand by me."

Mid-Life Marriage: Unique Challenges, Deliberate Choices

By mid-life, most marriages have weathered a fair amount of struggle and transition. Usually they are neither totally blissful nor completely without hope. In the muddled middle years, though, they are tested again and again by challenges unique to this season of life.

It takes emotional energy and sensitivity to know how to help Mom and Dad cope, or what boundaries are appropriate for boomerang kids. And, if you and your spouse can't agree on what to do, new tensions can stack up between you like dry kindling waiting to ignite. More tensions are added to the pile with fears of downsizing, financial crises, health scares, concerns over losing sexual attractiveness, and relinquishing youthful dreams.

No wonder we women have a driving passion at mid-life to experience a close, lasting, and fulfilling relationship. We want and need to be cherished. We thirst to be heard for who we are, held with genuine love, and helped in our weakness or confusion. And we are not alone. Our spouse also needs this deep and growing relationship as we move together into uncharted waters.

To recycle a stagnant and crumbling marriage into one that is mutually satisfying requires a deliberate effort by both partners. You can appeal to your husband, but you can't force him to change. You can only change one person—yourself. Are you willing to make the effort, even at the cost of choosing different thought patterns, verbal responses, and behavior?

Solomon vividly describes our choices as women during this time in life: becoming a wise woman who builds her house, or a foolish woman who tears it down with her own hands.[3] Choose to be wise and focus on renewing your commitment and building your marriage. Here are some essential component for success:

Accept Your Differences. Some of your husband's irritating habits may never change. Learn to look the other way. It may help to remember your own shortcomings.

Accept the fact that if certain expectations, needs, or dreams haven't yet materialized in your marriage, they probably aren't going to. Years ago, I dreamed of having long, late-night discussions with my husband over a cup of coffee on everything from ethics to the deeper meaning of the minor prophets. Too late I discovered I'd married a man who doesn't even like coffee and who needs his sleep! I've told myself, "That's life. Accept it."

Learn to Compromise. Being married to a strong-willed man is hard when you're a strong-willed woman—especially one who knows her way is best! In the early years of our marriage, sparks often flew when I didn't get my way. Now that the years have mellowed me, I value the bonding power of compromise. Instead of dueling to the death or withdrawing into silence, remember your goal: to have a growing and healthy relationship.

In their seminar "How to Have a Good Fight,"[4] Doug and Joyce Wachsmuth suggest husbands and wives rate on a scale of one to ten how important an issue is to each of them. The one to whom the issue is least important gives way to the one with stronger feelings. This certainly isn't foolproof, and can be abused by either partner, but done with love it helps build two important ingredients in a marriage: respect and consideration.

Communicate Clearly. A husband is not a mind reader, no matter how many years the two of you have shared the same bed. Crying to your girlfriend, "He should know what's the matter by now," won't make it any clearer to him.

In her bestselling book on male-female communication *You Just Don't Understand*,[5] Deborah Tannen points out that women need to process their thoughts and feelings through talking, but a man prefers brief, factual exchanges of information. So if you have a need for understanding or to be listened to but not given precise instructions on how to solve your problems, do yourself a favor: tell him what you want in nonemotional tones and, most important, without elaboration.

If your husband happens to be the emotional, talkative type, ignore this information.

Concentrate on the Positive. A renewed commitment to your spouse can come only from renewed thinking about him. You may think your husband has failed and hurt you, but if you are committed to building your relationship, start evaluating how you think about him. Do you view him negatively or call him names in your mind? Have you labeled him?

In Philippians 4:8, Paul gives us a marriage-building mindset: Think about whatever is true of your husband, whatever is noble and right and pure. Focus on what is lovely and admirable about him. Recall what is excellent or praiseworthy and share with him the positive qualities you see. Then, whenever that critical spirit reappears, repeat the process.

Rekindling the Flame

One wife from Texas advised caution as she described how she and her husband kept the love-sparks flashing between them. In a letter to a well-known advice columnist, she said they had showered together since they were newlyweds. However, one evening, when they were both in the shower, she dropped the soap. Her husband bent over to get it, slipped, hit his head on the water faucet, cutting a gash in his scalp, and ended up in the emergency room with eighteen stitches. Her final comment: We still shower together—but very, very carefully.

Rekindling the flame at mid-life is critical, but it takes determination to maintain a level of fun and creativity. Do you—or your husband—really want to settle for a boring peck on the cheek when your hormones are calling for more? Probably not. But when you factor in exhaustion, anxiety, or a lifestyle guaranteed to wear out the Energizer bunny, it's easy to see why many couples live as if their batteries are dead or dying.

A sterile and routine marriage is ripe for invasion by a younger or more fun-loving person who promises life, vibrancy, and excitement (and years of regrets). The fact that two out of three second marriages fail is incentive enough for feeding the flame you have right now.

Another land mine waiting to destroy a dull marriage is the rising frustration level of one partner with the status quo. Women are especially vulnerable to the call of our culture to strike out on their own and refuse to put up with a man who makes no effort to improve the relationship.

Divorce is not, however, God's answer to a dull or unhappy marriage.[6] Not only is it less than His design for us, divorce is also a source of pain and poverty for many women. Wanting to avoid divorce honors God and makes practical sense, so let's look at what you can do to keep your marriage alive and thriving both now and in the future.

Be Attractive to Your Husband. This does not mean you have to be a size six. We are all built differently and mid-life does some strange things to once-girlish figures. As my friend Janice said, "I have everything I had twenty years ago, but now it's all lower."

Maybe for you it's bigger or lumpier or reshaped, but the essential question is, what does your husband find attractive in a woman? Do the best you can with your body: exercise it, nourish it, give it plenty of sleep. Color your gray hair, experiment with new makeup, buy a new outfit. Whatever makes you feel more attractive to your husband . . . pursue it. But be sure you are reading him right: Does he like a woman who follows politics? Who reads the comics? Who shares his interest in computers or gardening or the home team? If you feel secure in your relationship, ask your husband what qualities he most enjoys in the women he works with or others you both know. On the other hand, if either of you is prone to jealousy or suspicion, leave that subject alone.

Be Affectionate. Pamela's face broke into a broad smile as she described how she trained her husband to express affection. "John came from an undemonstrative family," she explained. "Their way of showing love was to shake hands when they met, even if they hadn't seen each other for years. I knew I had to do something if I wanted to be hugged and kissed outside of the bedroom."

John always gave Pamela a kiss when he returned home at night, so she capitalized on the opportunity. "I would ask him to put his briefcase down and wrap his arms around me," she said. "Then I'd say 'squeeze me,' and 'squeeze me some more.' Before long he realized that I needed more than a quick smack on the lips. He also learned that I wasn't asking for anything more, at least not right then."

Affection sweetens and deepens the bond between you and your husband. Give him a caress as you pass, or a kiss for no reason other than that you are physically near him. Put an arm around his waist or snuggle up beside him during a game on TV and stroke his leg (but don't expect him to stop watching the game).

Forget about acting your age. Instead, develop your more playful, childlike side by loosening up your personality, your body language, your appearance, and your attitude. Make sure being with you is fun. Express affection physically and verbally, and your husband will celebrate his good fortune to have married YOU.

Be Appreciative. "When our children were young," reminisced Paula, "I used to teach them to say, 'Thank you, Daddy,' whenever we took them out for pizza or ice cream. I wanted them to grow up noticing and appreciating all their blessings."

Looking down shyly, Paula continued, "I try to thank Jack whenever I notice his little acts of kindness. After twenty years of marriage, it's so easy to take each other for granted. It doesn't take much effort to express appreciation, even for routine chores like his putting out the weekly garbage or keeping up the yard."

When Paula affirms and appreciates her husband, she is practicing a powerful principle for building a successful relationship. This is not a new truth. In fact, Jesus taught it long ago when he said, "Do to others what you would have them do to you."[7] Ask yourself:

Do I like to be appreciated for what I do and who I am?

Does encouragement lift me up?

Am I motivated by a word or gesture of thanks?

If he doesn't say the things you long to hear, look for what he quietly does for you. For a thriving relationship, sprinkle your husband liberally with doses of appreciation and get ready to enjoy the results. He may even start thanking you for those little acts of love by paying more attention to his part in the marriage.

Be Alert to His Feelings. "A woman needs a man like a fish needs a bicycle," trumpets one bumper-sticker. Male-bashing is a popular sport, even among some Christian women. Bombarded with images of the "ugly man" who batters his wife, makes sexist remarks, or walks away from his responsibilities, many women now view men suspiciously and quickly react to perceived insults. Not even their long-time husbands escape this cultural reeducation.

In contrast to the ugly-man image that permeates our culture, the Christian community also has its male image that bombards our minds. This man is called the "perfect Christian husband." He is expected to be attentive to you, sensitive to your needs, and expressive of his feelings. Anything less than this and he is called a failure. Little wonder many men feel they never measure up.

Your spouse probably stands somewhere between the ugly man and the perfect Christian husband. He has times of feeling tired, overwhelmed, or inadequate as a father and husband. Perhaps he struggles to meet your spiritual, emotional, or material expectations, but knows he falls far short.

Choosing to be alert and concerned about your husband's feelings is a powerful way to express love. It is also vital for developing closeness in the years ahead. To strengthen the bonds between you, try observing your husband thoughtfully. Watch his expression and body language as he talks. Listen, without interrupting, when he expresses his feelings or reactions, being alert for opportunities to affirm and encourage. In addition, as you pray for him, ask God to give you new insights into the feelings of this unique individual. Remember, men may hide their feelings more than women, but they still have them!

Rekindling the mid-life marriage takes persistence and determination. Love never asks, "How much *must* I do?" but rather, "How much *can* I do?" What are you willing to do now to splash the canvas of your relationship with vibrant colors of laughter, caring, and growing contentment? If you'll boldly revisit your marriage, renew your commitment, and rekindle that spark, you won't ever have to ask, "Will you still love me when I'm . . . ?"

A sizzling marriage in the early years—and sometimes the later years, too—frequently leads to a common result: little look-alikes of you and your hubby start appearing around the house. Inevitably, these little look-alikes grow up and make life stressful by refusing to act and dress like your offspring! Then, one day, they wave goodbye.

Now what do you do? How do you relate to these former youngsters now masquerading as adults? What do you do when you find yourself muttering into thin air, "These children are too old to be mine"? Let's find out.

5

These Children Are
Too Old to Be Mine

"Hi, Mom! Hi, Dad!" Our two children, Malaika and Elliot, crowded through the front door. Their exuberance lit up the house as they struggled to hold on to presents, coats, bags, and ski poles and reach out for hugs at the same time. Driving together from Seattle to Portland, they were excited to come home from college for the Christmas break.

Anticipating this scene in my mind all day, I had imagined rushing forward to greet them. Instead, for a brief second I stood frozen in amazement. *Who are these people?*

They're so tall, so adult. How did they change so quickly? Are these my children? How can they be? They're too old to be mine!

The powerful realization that Malaika and Elliot were now adults startled me. Later, in a quiet moment, I thought back to a scene just a few years before.

Striding confidently toward us, hand extended to grab Malaika's duffel bag, a handsome college senior welcomed us to freshman orientation weekend. "What's your name?" he asked, looking at Malaika.

The mother's heart in me sank as I heard a squeaky, frightened voice barely respond. "My name's Malaika," said my normally warm, outgoing daughter. Suddenly, our poised, ready-for-anything masks were ripped off, exposing the emotions we had both tried to deny. Malaika was scared, and so was I.

Stumbling through the rest of the weekend, I dabbed at ever-flowing tears and wrestled with dark, depressing thoughts. How could I bear to drive home and leave Malaika scared and alone? Could she cope with none of her high-school friends around; could she keep up academically; would she eat properly and get enough sleep? How would she manage without ME? . . . How would I manage without her?

Watching Malaika take those first steps into her own life had been emotionally wrenching but vitally necessary. To develop into the person God intended, she had to leave the safe harbor of home and launch into adulthood. Now, filled with joy and the wonder of discovery, I realized that my once frightened teenager had indeed blossomed into a mature young woman eager to give her mom a hug.

Independence Is God's Plan

When the nest begins to empty, life changes. That adorable silky-skinned little baby, once crying to be held and then contentedly nuzzling against your cheek, now needs and craves freedom to explore life on its own. A child, like a butterfly bursting through its cocoon, obeys the urge God gave to break free.

Peggy Altig, a family counselor from Portland, Oregon, summarizes this familiar struggle. "Learning to be a separate person is the main task of young adulthood, becoming equal rather than being under the parent's dominance," she says. In contrast, the main task we parents face is letting go and releasing control. It isn't as easy as we might think.

Seated at an overloaded Thanksgiving table, Elliot ate like a starved wolf. Jim and I had looked forward to his first visit home from college and were full of questions. During a lull in the conversation Elliot turned to me, drumstick in hand, and said, "All the guys on our floor in the dorm are going to get an earring." With an impish smile he inquired, "What do you think, Mom?"

"Not if you want your tuition paid, you're not," I shot back. So much for releasing control and encouraging freedom.

Parental control, so necessary at certain stages of our child's development, can be a hard habit to break, but it must be done. Giving our children-turned-young-adults freedom to make their own decisions is tough for many of us.

Why is this? Why do we tug on the ropes that bind them to us, when they long to be respected as individuals with their own opinions, capable of running their own lives? Why do many moms in the muddled middle years find it so difficult to transition from a mother-child to a mother-friend relationship? Let's find out.

What's Behind a Mom's Struggles?

Loss of Identity and Purpose

For many mothers, the emptying nest ushers in as profound a life change as retirement after a lifelong career. "I don't know who I am anymore," said Marcia in an anguished voice. "I spent my time being a room mother, ferrying the kids to sports activities, doing fund-raisers, and just being a mom. Now who am I? What am I supposed to do?"

Marcia's sense of being needed went out the door along with the last of her children. Her primary identity as a mom was gone, and so was her sense of purpose and direction. The comfortable routine of family life, from cooking large-sized casseroles to washing loads of laundry, changed forever. Having few other sources of fulfillment in her life, Marcia felt heartbroken and lost when the nest emptied.

Do you share some of Marcia's struggles? With the empty nest looming or already here, do you have a feeling of hollowness? How can you and I survive and thrive in this difficult stage?

First, *remember that this period of your family life is a transition*—and as such is bound to be a bittersweet time. Be gentle with yourself. Take time to grieve and reminisce. After all, you are experiencing a loss of the familiar and trading one form of family life for something yet unknown.

Another part of the answer is to *start thinking of yourself in terms other than "mother."* Your role is undergoing major remodeling. Who *are* you, in addition to being your child's parent? It will take time to discover a fresh identity, one that fits who you are becoming at this stage of your life. To uncover these hidden facets of who you are requires actively expanding your horizons, building on who you have become over the past years. Later chapters will address this process in more detail.

Meanwhile, what is the likely result? After a time, feelings of dislocation and loss begin to diminish. You start realizing that not only have you survived this bittersweet transition but you have also come to enjoy an adult-to-adult relationship with your children. Plus, you now cherish your freedom to explore the next stage of your own life.

Loosening of the Mother-Child Bond

Another mom, who is also a full-time counselor, looked ahead a few years and sighed, "I love my boys so much, I can't imagine what it will be like when they're gone." Most of us moms, whether contentedly at home full time or out in the marketplace, share these feelings—at least on the good days.

Loving our children and being loved by them is what God intended. This love—a tough, flexible bond—knits the family together despite the clashes, power struggles, and hurtful words that often mark the teenage years.

However, no matter how much we love our children, they are essentially on loan from God. They are ours to nurture, shape, and guide for a short period of time. We don't own them or have the right to live their lives for them. Our task is to prepare them for life. Then, whether we feel they are ready or not, we surround them with prayer and release them into their own separate worlds.

The Fear Factor

Waking up in the night, Vicky wrestled with her fears. What if Jon falls in with the wrong crowd? What if he can't hold a job? What if he rejects all we've sought to instill in him?

Watching our children step into a separate world can be very frightening. Because we love them so much and care about their well-being, it's easy to imagine all the difficulties they might face and wonder if they'll be able to cope. The temptation to control, push, or manipulate can become overwhelming when we focus on all that could go wrong. No wonder we want to charge in and rescue. If we don't help our precious baby, who will?

Often, layered beneath these genuine concerns for our children, lurk our own unexamined fears and twisted beliefs. You may recognize some of these:

If my child chooses behavior I don't approve of, it must mean I've failed as a parent.

If my child is less than perfect, people in my church and family will look down on me.

If my child doesn't do as well as my friends' children, I'll look bad and be embarrassed.

In their insightful book *What Did I Do Wrong? Practical Help for Parents Who Think Its Too Late,*[1] William and Candace Backus tackle common misbeliefs about parenting. They suggest you stop and question twisted thoughts that gnaw away at your peace. Ask yourself:

Why am I fearful? Why do I feel guilty? Why do I feel responsible?

What am I telling myself that makes me feel like this? Is
it true or logical?

How am I responsible for my grown child's choices?

After recognizing the link between her distorted
thoughts and the feelings of fear that gripped her whenever she thought of Jon, Vicky decided to take charge of
her thinking. "Now, when I wake in the night," she said, "I
pray for Jon and commit him into God's care. I also make
a conscious effort to remember Jon is capable of making
his own decisions and he'll learn from his mistakes, just
as I had to."

Like Vicky, all of us want our children to march through
life without going down dead-end roads or destructive paths.
We dread the thought of our unmarried daughters getting
pregnant or our sons becoming addicted to alcohol or drugs.
Having lived many years longer than they have, we know the
damage that follows certain choices. Hard as it is, however,
we have to stand back, give advice only if asked, and let them
choose their own paths.

You aren't responsible for their choices. During those mo-
ments that you feel you are, ask yourself: "When am I, then,
not responsible? When my child is thirty, forty-five, sixty?
Why not eighteen?"

Not only can you not make choices for your children,
it isn't your job to shield them from painful consequences.
Stepping in to fix an adult child's problem robs them of taking
responsibility for their own actions. This in turn delays their
progress toward adult maturity.

When you are overwhelmed with the desire to save your
child from the suffering that results from bad choices, take

heart. God uses both good results and hard consequences as life-shaping tools.

If hands-on control is out, what does that leave us to do? Pray daily, load on encouragement and affirmation when appropriate, treat these emerging adults as friends, and consciously trust God to work. After this, there's one more step to take: rip off your "I'm a perfect mother with a perfect child" mask. Untie yourself from the fear of what others think. What difference does it make, really?

Thinking of God's acceptance of you while you were yet a sinner (Rom. 5:8) will produce the courage you need to be honest with yourself and others. This is part of our own growth process. Who knows—maybe God will use your appropriate openness and vulnerability to bring hope to another struggling mom.

Many of us moms have a hard time launching our children into the world. But have you ever wondered what feelings your kids wrestle with? Do you struggle to understand what's behind the way they react? Do you wish you could peer into their minds and figure them out? Let's try to look at some of their core needs and how we can respond to them.

What's Behind My Child's Struggles?

Give Me Liberty or Give Me Death

Patrick Henry's famous statement could well describe the internal drive of every young adult. They must fly from the nest. They must become a separate person if a healthy sense of self is to develop.

The drive to be a separate and independent person begins long before a child is mature enough to make wise decisions, as we've all experienced. Little Jimmy refuses to hold Mom's hand crossing the street because "I'm a big boy now." Later he demands to have his initials carved into his buzz haircut, despite your pleas for something less radical. He groans at going on vacation with the family and wonders why he can't take care of his fifteen-year-old self at home for a week. He refuses to go to the mall with you—unless *you're* buying what *he* picks, of course.

During the time of late adolescence, answers to three crucial questions are being worked out.[2] Who am I? How do I relate to others? What should I believe? Moody, rebellious attitudes or behavior that sends you running for a jug of antacid are surface clues to normal teenage anxieties and tensions that accompany moving from one developmental stage to the next. Their inner propulsion to become a separate, unique person is not meant as a personal rejection of you (at least, not permanently), but is a response to God's programming.

Much as you want to, don't squeeze your child into your own mold. Grant them freedom to be different from you.

Peggy Altig, a family counselor and mother of three teenagers, advises, "The ultimate goal in releasing our children is having them replace external, parental control with internal self-control. The sooner we give them choices within choices with safe consequences, we strengthen their ability to make wise decisions. By saying, 'You decide—these are the consequences of each of these choices,' they can learn that if they want good outcomes, they must make good decisions. It's better to let them learn through less serious decisions while at home than more risky ones when on their own."

As moms going through our own struggles to release, we need to weigh carefully the issues we'll take a stand on. Remember, we want to be friends with our adult kids, even if they don't dress like us, think like us, or behave like us. After all, do you dress, think, and behave like your parents?

Please Listen to Me

"I hear what you're saying, and the answer is no."
"Don't tell me, I know what you're going to say."
"I don't care what the circumstances are, you're not going."

Do any of these statements sound familiar? What do they have in common? They're usually said to our kids with steam billowing from our nostrils and eyes glaring like laser beams. Exasperation, frustration, and anger erupt, and communication comes to a screeching halt. Too late we realize we've once again responded without a moment's reflection on the emotions, needs, and longings behind our child's words. What follows? Walls of silence go up or short, clipped sentences replace free-flowing conversation, and a sickening feeling of alienation and hopelessness floods in.

Authors William and Candace Backus believe that one of the major mistakes we parents make is in how we communicate with our children. They suggest that rather than telling our children what WE want THEM to hear, we need to *listen* to what they are trying to say to us.

What are some bad "hearing habits" we need to discard so our children will feel heard?

Defensiveness: I'm not to blame, you made me . . .
Control: You'd better do what I say, or else . . .
Criticism: You have no idea about the value of money.
Ridicule: What do you know about anything?
Sarcasm: Right, you're so clever aren't you. . . .

Rather than arguing, giving orders, or refusing to listen, try to hear beneath the surface. Here are more helpful ways to meet your child's need to be heard:

Look for what's not being said. What feelings lie behind their words and body language?

Don't debate their opinions. Without interrogating them, ask how they came to their view and why they hold it. Show respect for their ideas while being free to say you don't share them.

Check out signs of anger. If they seem angry, ask them why—and listen to their answer without resorting to bad "hearing habits."

Be willing to ask, "How have I hurt you?"

"A gentle answer turns away wrath,"[3] wrote Solomon. In the heat and tension that can develop between us and our young adult children, it's easy to forget the power of quiet, loving, and caring words. Do your kids complain, "Mom, you never listen?" or, "Mom, you always think you're right—you always have to have the last word." Is it time for you to apologize and listen?

Do You Believe in Me?

What is it that puts zing and hope into our steps as women in mid-life, peering into the future and wondering what lies ahead? What gives our kids confidence as they stand at the brink of adult life? Whether moms or young adults, the answer is the same: regular doses of reassurance that we are loved, we are capable, and we'll make it in life.

If these power-packed emotional vitamins give *us* strength, imagine their impact on our kids. Letting them know that you believe in them is a gift you can give again and again, and it doesn't even cost money! Here are some ways to say I believe in you:

Practice Smiling. Check what your face automatically does when your young adult starts with a "Mom, could you . . ." Does your brow furrow up? Do your lips glue themselves into a straight line? If you have the usual number of mother-child confrontations, the answer is probably yes. Corny as it sounds, try a smile. Smile when you see them. Smile as you listen without interrupting. Smile genuinely as you respond. Not only will your own mood be better, but once your child gets over the shock, your relationship with each other will run smoother.

Ask Their Opinion. Do you ask your husband for his opinions and advice? Do you ask friends? How about your adult child? Asking someone their opinion sends a message: "I believe in you and value what you think." Treating our kids with the same respect we give to other adults makes a powerful statement. We are saying, "I see you as an individual with your own views, and I want to hear them." Their opinions might shock or dismay you. On the other hand, you will know what they're thinking and dealing with in today's world.

Be Affirming. Some mothers are naturally warm and fuzzy, full of kind and loving comments to their children. But there's hope for the rest of us.

The help we need begins in our prayer life. Instead of praying our fears and reinforcing them in our minds, pray in faith. Claim the Bible's promises that God will watch over and work in your child's life by thanking Him for what He is doing now—in secret.[4] Ask God to help you focus on your children's good points. Then write down those positive traits in a prayer journal as a reminder. Finally, verbalize them to your child. Tell your son you appreciate his thrift. Or his honesty—even if his truth-telling hurts at times. Praise your daughter's determination to pay off her credit card charges every month, her choice of friends, or her hard work.

When you see marks of maturity, say something. Verbal affirmation is like plant food: pour it on regularly, then stand back and watch the blooming begin.

Express Confidence. In the musical *My Fair Lady*, Professor Higgins believed he could successfully turn Cockney flower-seller Eliza Doolittle into a lady fit for English society. And he did. Calling this the Pygmalion effect, researchers have conducted similar experiments. What have they discovered? Interestingly, studies show that when we believe something about another person, we unconsciously say and do things that cause that belief to become reality. As a result, when confidence is expressed in someone, that person frequently exceeds all previous expectations.

What does this say to us moms? Express confidence in your child! Whether debating what to do about school, where to live, or what job to take, tell them you believe in their ability to make good decisions. When they head off to the other side of the world to see what's there, tell them you believe they are capable of taking care of themselves. At every opportunity, let them know you're confident they will come through the young-adult passage successfully.

Shifting Gears: From Mother-Child to Mother-Friend

Growing up, our children lived under our roof and benefited from our provision for their needs. Now that they are young adults, the time has come to shift from the outgrown *mother-dependent* child mode to an emotionally healthy *mother-friend* mode.

Changing from our "provider-and-protector-against-the-world" mindset, however, isn't easy. Nor is letting go of what we have grown so accustomed to: being in charge. How can we think of giving up the power to utter those immortal words: "Because I'm your mother, that's why"?

Instead of following old patterns of bossing and commanding, controlling and prying, we must try new ways of interacting with our kids. What are we aiming at in this evolving mother-child bond? Isn't it to nurture and shape something lasting and precious that has not existed up till now? Our goal is nothing less than an adult-to-adult, friend-to-friend, equal-to-equal relationship between ourselves and our grown child.

The road to this worthy end is rarely smooth. To get there we need to be tough with ourselves and our offspring, setting up boundaries that are clear and fair to both them and us.

Boundaries

Home, Sweet Home

"Marilee is moving home after her college graduation," said her mother, Carolyn, raising her eyebrows in resignation. "I'm not sure returning to the nest is the best thing for her, but she wants to come home."

Choosing to live with parents is widespread among young adults in our culture. Whether the reasons for this are limited finances, insecurity, or the comforts of home (surely Mom still cooks, cleans, and does laundry), having grown kids live at home calls for a family conference. Be sure to discuss:

Length of Stay. To avoid prolonged dependency and stunted personal growth, allow your child to stay with you only until they can make better arrangements. Set a time limit. Don't be embarrassed to ask them to pay close to what they would pay for room and board elsewhere. Your goal is to gently but firmly move them out on their own. Nobody else will give free rent.

The mother eagle lines her nest with feathers. Then, when the time comes for her young to stretch their wings and fly, she deliberately makes the nest uncomfortable by pulling the feathers out. If you want your young adult to fly, remove his feather bed, but be prepared for some squawking.

House Courtesy Rules. Remember the house is yours. Set down the same rules you would for a boarder. If you expect to be called when they're not coming home for meals or for the night, say so. Lay out the moral standards you expect them to abide by in your home. You can't control what they do away from home, but you can uphold your standards in your own home.

What's Mine Is Not Yours. Despite what your child might think, what's yours does not belong to them. Teach them that adults purchase their own possessions.

Don't feel guilty about setting rules for how your belongings are used. Expect them to leave the gas tank as full as you left it, to pay insurance, and to cover the deductible if there's an accident. If they break or lose something, let them know adult behavior will be expected of them, that is, they will replace it.

Financial Boundaries

Don't bail your kid out of natural consequences. If you overdraw at the bank, who bails you out? Control your tendency to come to their financial rescue. If you don't, rather than paying off their debts or saving for next week's expenses, your daughter will keep getting her nails done and your son will continue buying sports equipment. If they need money, encourage them to visit their friendly banker and take out a loan. Repaying the bank carries a lot more weight than repaying good ol' Mom or Dad.

Check out when your child goes off your health insurance policy. If they refuse to pay for their own insurance, don't protect them from the consequences of their choice. Remember, your goal is to support them emotionally on their journey to becoming self-sufficient adults, not float them financially whenever they're in need. Yes, you will worry when they make poor choices, but God has a big lap—dump your worries there.

Relating as Adult to Adult

Once you were needed to fix things. You kissed bumps and bruises all better, refereed fights, assigned chores, and made arrangements to keep your offspring occupied and out of trouble. None of that is needed anymore. Your role has changed. Tell your young adult, "If you want help, ask me." And then stay out of their affairs. Get a life of your own.

When your young adult asks you for help, give options rather than solutions. Explore their thinking but let them decide. Tell them they are the authors of their lives and the consequences are their responsibility, and then *drop it*.

Be interested in what they enjoy doing and invite them to activities they would like. They'll also appreciate you making an effort to welcome their friends. If this is tough, try remembering that God doesn't look on the outside.[5] Work hard to love your kids unconditionally, and pray for help to separate their passing behavior from who they are.

Be encouraged. According to experts, the need to separate and be different—even to rebel—eventually mellows out. Around age thirty, most adult children begin to return to the values they were raised with.

Just imagine, one day we might actually hear them softly groan, "Oh no, I've turned out just like my mom." I'm already smiling in delicious anticipation.

Launching adult kids is a major energy-zapper. But stock up on your high-potency vitamins and double your exercise routine: your parents also need thought and attention during this season of life. How are they doing? Are they prepared for their future? Are you? Let's think about how to help them if and when they need it.

6

My Parents Need Me—
How Should I Help?

"Poppy, it's Dad," said a deep voice, trembling with emotion. The phone line between Peterborough, England, and Portland, Oregon, was so clear I could hear my father suck in his breath before continuing. "Mum had a heart attack three days ago, and we were sure she'd recover, so we didn't call you. I'm sorry we didn't, but we wanted to keep you from worrying when you're so far away."

"Oh, Dad," I gasped, feeling as if a karate chop had smacked me in the stomach. "Is she alive?"

"Yes, but the doctor just told us she's developed complications. She isn't expected to live. Can you come?"

Barely able to speak, I said, "Yes, Dad. I'll get a ticket and try to be on the Seattle-London flight this afternoon. I'll call you as soon as I arrive in England."

I hung up the phone, overwhelmed by the agonizing awareness that my mother was dying. Turning toward my husband, I sobbed out the news as he held me close.

"It's Saturday morning," Jim said when I calmed down. "I don't know if any travel agents are open, but I'll try to find you a ticket and some traveler's checks."

At that moment, I remembered—I couldn't leave the country. "My immigration card!" I cried. "I lost it months ago and haven't applied for a new one."

Holding on to my British citizenship while living in America gave me a feeling of connection with my roots. But it also meant I couldn't reenter the States without my permanent resident card. I was stuck.

Wailing, "I can't leave because I can't get back into the country," a thought occurred to me. A voice seemed to say, *Look in your passport.* Crossing quickly to the desk, I pulled open the drawer containing our passports, grabbed mine, and shook it. Out floated my immigration card.

In His gentle yet powerful way, God reminded me I wasn't walking through this painful passage alone, a truth that's easy to forget when you are in shock or crisis.

A few hours later came another reminder. Waiting for my seat assignment before boarding the flight from Seattle, I prayed about whether to explain my situation and ask for an empty row, if such a thing existed. I dreaded the thought of sitting with happy, chatty tourists wanting to know why I was visiting London. Deciding against this, I prayed for God to take care of the situation.

My heart sank on finding my assigned seat—it was in a fully booked section next to the smoking area. Everyone seemed ready to party. When I prayed again, a few minutes later a flight attendant came by. This time I spoke up, asking if I could be moved to a seat away from the smoking section. Promising to do her best she soon returned, leading me to an empty row of seats. Sitting down, I closed my tear-filled eyes and thanked God for His kindness.

A short time later, I noticed a plaque on the side of the galley and read it with awe. Unknown to me, British Airways names their planes after English cities and my plane was called *The City of Peterborough*. Home! I stared at the plaque in amazement as the words of Jesus flooded over me with fresh power, "Lo, I am with you always."

As the tabernacle in the middle of the camp reminded the Israelites of God's presence, the plaque forced me to remember that nothing, not even my lonely journey, escaped God's attention. He knew where I was going. He knew why. I felt Him saying, "Poppy, you're not alone. I'll be with you through all that lies ahead. I'll provide all you'll need."

After flying through the night, I arrived at Peterborough Hospital twenty-four hours after Dad's phone call. Gathered around Mum's bed, my father and sisters tried to control their grief.

Drawing close, I gently stroked my mother's hair, whispering, "Mum, it's Poppy."

Hearing my voice, she opened her eyes and looked at me. "Poppy, I'm dying," she said, her voice barely audible.

"I know, Mum," I choked out. "I've come to be with you."

Staying with her through the night, I watched as my formerly passionate, feisty, funny mother slipped into a coma. She died early the next morning. Mum was only seventy years old.

Death at seventy. That's too young by today's standards. Thanks to medical advances and a determination to squeeze the most out of life, many of today's seventy-year-olds enjoy a lifestyle more typical of fifty-year-olds three decades ago.

My friend Dottie, a lively and active seventy-nine-year-old, vividly illustrates this zesty approach to aging. She wants to celebrate her upcoming eightieth birthday with pizzazz! How could she do it? How could she ever top her skydiving debut at seventy-five? By Bungee-jumping?

Life expectancy has increased dramatically in this century, presenting society as a whole with entirely new challenges. In contrast to an average lifespan of fifty years in 1900, in the mid-'90s life expectancy was seventy-two years for men and seventy-nine years for women.

Not only are seniors living longer, their numbers are also rapidly increasing. According to Census Bureau estimates, by the year 2000 there were about thirty-five million Americans aged sixty-five or older, and by 2010 there will be forty million. In fact, the fastest growing segment of the elderly population is the over-eighty-five-year-olds, and even the ranks of those over one hundred years swell year by year.

As women in the middle years, often "sandwiched" between growing children and aging parents, these statistics seem to us like a double-edged sword. On the one hand, we're grateful our parents will live longer, and hope they'll enjoy their golden years. On the other hand, women who want to lovingly care for their elderly parents struggle with the additional responsibility.

Many studies point out that three-quarters of all caregivers to the elderly are married women in the middle years or older. After raising their own children, a large number will assist their aging parents for varying lengths of time. Fortunately, there are a growing number of support systems available.

Coping With Reality

"Dad was diagnosed with dementia and Alzheimer's last year at eighty-eight," said Joan, a bubbly fifty-two-year-old, over lunch. "He and Mom were very independent until then, but Dad has deteriorated rapidly in the last few months. Mom feels so guilty that she isn't able to care for him herself, but she doesn't have the strength to do it.

"Dad can't sleep at night so he gets up and tries to leave the house, and then he gets belligerent when she tries to stop him. Sometimes he confuses a corner of the bedroom for the bathroom."

Shaking her head, she continued, "There's no way Mom can manage without live-in help, and even that is a temporary situation. We're having to look for respite care, an Alzheimer's group, and even a nursing home for Dad. Where Mom will live if Dad goes into a home is another issue we have to discuss."

Joan lives an hour's drive away from her parents, has a full-time job, a husband, and a school-age child. Fortunately, a widowed relative who lives near her parents has assured Joan that she will visit her parents often. "God has given me your folks as my ministry," she says.

Joan goes to see her mother and father one day a week and talks to them almost daily.

Listening to her story, I mused, "What are my kids going to do with me when I'm no longer able to take care of myself?"

When I teasingly posed this question to my son, he didn't hesitate to reassure me of his devotion. "Don't worry, Mom," he said. "We'll stick you in a nursing home and visit once a year!" I trust he was being funny.

Be Prepared

The Boy Scout motto, *Be Prepared*, is good advice for women in their middle years. You don't have to live in fear of the negative. But, you do need to make time to prayerfully assess how you and your family will cope when your parents need help.

The first step in being prepared is to ask yourself some hard questions:

How do I honestly feel about this opportunity God has given me to honor my parents?

How can I care for them, if necessary, *and* take care of myself and my family at the same time? What changes in my schedule will be required?

How can I help preserve their self-respect if they become more dependent and need assistance?

What will I be modeling to my children by my response? Is it how I would want them to treat me?

If I should find myself more involved in my parents' lives, are there any barriers between us I need to take down?

Whether you feel fiery devotion or a guilty sense of duty at the thought of taking care of your parents, you need to know what to expect and what to do. Being prepared means learning as much as possible about the challenges that may lie ahead. For more extensive and detailed information on the issues raised in this chapter, consult the Senior and Disabled Services office of your state Human Resources Division.

Be Prepared: Empathy Required

> People are changing. They are so much younger than they used to be when I was their age. On the other hand, people my own age are so much older than I am. I ran across an old classmate the other day, and he had aged so badly he didn't recognize me!
>
> —author unknown

While we laugh at denials of aging, they tell us something we need to keep in the forefront of our minds: No one loses independence and control without a struggle. Empathy, which the dictionary defines as "the capacity to participate in another's feelings or ideas from their point of view, not your own," is essential.

Put Yourself in Their Shoes

"Why can't I still drive?" demanded eighty-five-year-old Pearl, when her daughter Alice gently insisted it was time to give up the car keys. "If I go slowly enough I can get to the grocery store and back."

Unknown to her mother, Alice had followed her one morning as she drove to the supermarket. "I couldn't help admiring Mom's determination," she said, smiling at the memory. "She carefully inched along and didn't even notice the line of fuming drivers stuck behind her. I also solved the mystery of why her brakes had to be replaced every few months. Her brake lights were on for the entire trip!"

"I watched Mom's face as she processed what I told her," said Alice, grimacing. "She struggled with the thought of no longer getting into her car to run errands. Taking the local bus won't work when she wants to attend church or visit friends, and she's going to have to call someone even to get a quart of milk."

Not all older seniors lose their independence, however. Nor do they age at the same rate. Now in her nineties, Bertha Holt, founder of an adoption agency, runs every day. Another healthy eighty-three-year-old man exercises a half hour a day. He developed his routine twenty years ago following a heart attack. After working out, he spends the day driving around his ranch in a Jeep, fixing fences and admiring his cattle.

Positive role models fill every issue of *Modern Maturity*, a magazine for seniors, published by the American Association for Retired People (AARP).[1] From joining archeological digs to photographing zebra on the Serengeti Plains, today's elderly no longer fit out-of-date stereotypes.

By placing a high priority on exercise and mental stimulation, your parents might have sharper wits and greater energy than you do. I know my father has! Nearing eighty, he finishes *The Times* crossword puzzle before I've figured out the clues. When he visits from England, I head for bed long before him. In the morning, he's up, dressed, and eager to browse around the mall before I'm ready for the day.

Many elderly people, however, are not so spry. They experience physical and mental difficulties and need help.

"I don't know how Mom will react to being escorted to appointments," Alice continued. "I'm sure she'll feel like a child needing supervision. In a way, being dependent not only for transportation but later for your own physical care must make you feel like a helpless baby." Alice's voice cracked as she softly added, "To see life as you've known it slip away—it has to be terribly difficult."

It's crucial in our no-nonsense, make-the-best-decision-and-get-on-with-it world that you slow down and try to *feel* what your mom or dad is experiencing.

Alice listened to her mother's fears with empathy and love. They even cried together. "I wanted Mom to know I cared," she said. "When your life changes drastically, you need compassion and understanding from those you love."

Be Prepared: Take Practical Steps Now

Talk, Talk, Talk . . .

Awkward as it is to ask your parents how they want their affairs handled should they become unable to manage on their own, don't put it off. A difficult situation can quickly escalate into a family crisis if you have no idea of their plans and wishes.

Raising these issues while they are still active and independent is less threatening than waiting until a serious illness clouds the decision-making process. Happily, you might find they have beaten you to it and made their arrangements already—and that *they* are relieved to be able to talk about it.

Try opening up the subject by discussing what plans *you* have made medically, financially, and legally regarding *your own* future. In a relaxed manner, share how you feel about living wills, heroic medical intervention, and where you'd like to live if and when you are no longer independent. Then invite them to discuss their views and preferences.

Be certain to assure your parents of your love, and that you aren't trying to pry or take over their lives. If they react negatively, don't push. Watch for another opportunity, perhaps when a friend of theirs dies suddenly or faces a serious health problem.

Ultimately, your goal is to have specific information regarding your parent's plans and wishes. Here's what you need to find out:

Medical Care. Have they made a living will[2] or filled out an advance medical directive[3] specifying their wishes should they become unable to speak for themselves? Who do they want as their designated health care representative should end-of-life decisions need to be made? Do they want to be kept alive at all costs?

Financial Provision. How do they plan to pay for long-term care if they need it? Are they aware of Medicare? Do they know how to apply? Do they have supplemental health insurance?

Living Arrangements. Do they plan to stay in their home or to move, perhaps to a retirement community out-of-state? If so, who will care for them if they become incapacitated? How do they feel about the choices of nursing homes, adult foster-care, live-in help, and living with you? (Remember, you're gathering information, not signing on the dotted line.)

Legal Matters. Do they have an up-to-date will? Have they arranged their financial affairs to minimize taxes and maximize what is left to the surviving spouse or heirs? Who do they want as Power of Attorney to handle their finances if this becomes necessary?

Location of Documents. Where do they keep insurance policies? What about Medicare, military, investment, and tax records, as well as the mortgage and automobile title?

A geriatric specialist for a local hospital advises, "If possible, hold a family conference before wrenching decisions have to be made. Be ahead of the game by having some idea of what you will do if Mom breaks her hip or Dad gets Parkinson's disease. Having a plan is vital.

"Think of yourselves as a team. Include your parents as well as all the siblings," she adds, "even the black sheep of the family. Then nobody can say decisions were made without their input. Let your parents be the team leaders who problem-solve together. Everyone needs to hear Mom's or

Dad's wishes and accept their right to choose or reject your suggestions, unless this isn't feasible."

If you think your brother will try to force his solution on everyone else or your sister will sit in silence but spew criticism later, you might want to ask an objective person outside the family to help you devise that plan of action.

If your parent is hospitalized, the social worker or discharge planner can help. Other professionals you can call on are your pastor, the hospital chaplain, or a family counselor. Your state's Department of Aging can also refer your family to a consultant.

Encourage Their Independence

Many aging adults resist being helped. They want to do things by themselves, and so they should. Some however, prefer premature dependency as a way to garner attention and avoid personal responsibility.

"My mother-in-law, Madge, phones every week to find out when she can move out West and live with us," Kendra said, an exasperated edge to her voice. "She is perfectly healthy, but since being widowed five years ago, she has refused to make a life of her own. Madge relied on Harold, my father-in-law, for everything. She looked to him to solve her problems and take care of her. Now that he's gone, she doesn't know how to cope. My brother-in-law allowed her to move in with him and his wife, but her neediness is driving him crazy."

Larry, Kendra's husband, feels trapped between his seventy-year-old mother's constant pleas to live with them and his wife's fears for their relationship if she does.

Sharing problems with family and friends helps women cope with stress in their lives. Ironically, this healthy feminine trait can backfire. Some elderly women, molded by a lifelong habit of turning to others for assistance, label themselves as more needy and helpless than the facts show. By choosing premature dependence, they unknowingly put family relationships under severe strain.

"Learned helplessness" has been a ploy used by women for generations, and it does come in useful at times. If you shrink from discussing with your friendly mechanic the finer points of why your car engine leaks, or you pale at the thought of figuring out your income tax forms, you know what to do: Act perplexed and look for someone (usually from the opposite gender) to bail you out. As women in mid-life, we'd be wise to remember that this "helpless female" mentality has a sting in its tail. If you don't want to end up prematurely dependent on others, start tackling life's difficult twists and turns by reminding yourself, "I'm a woman. I'm an adult. I can do it." (But, I have to confess, it sure is nice to have someone around to help.)

Whether male or female, the elderly benefit by staying in their homes, making their own decisions, and maintaining social contacts and interests for as long as possible. To encourage parents to stay independent, don't step in and do something if you think they can do it themselves. Instead, lovingly urge them to keep trying, but be ready to assist if necessary. Problem-solving together might be all that's needed.

If they want your help, you can accident-proof their house, explore home-care services, and check into community resources with them. By giving your mother and father practical support, they will be able to enjoy their independence for a longer time.

Be Prepared: Decide What You Can Do Best

Count the Cost

If you're going to build a tower or go to war, Jesus said, sit down and count the cost beforehand.[4] This wise advice certainly applies to taking a parent into your home.

Before you and your family make that decision, pray for wisdom and talk at length with a social worker or someone in the geriatric field. After finding out what might be required, sit down with your husband and other family members and evaluate your resources. Then, before you get immersed in the actual care of your parent, stop and make plans to keep yourself healthy and your life balanced. Taking a parent into your home affects many lives, so let's take a closer look at three steps that can help.

Pray Without Ceasing

Ask God if this is His solution. Bring Him your fears about taking care of your mom or dad, and confess any feelings of resentment or guilt that well up. If there are unresolved issues between you and a parent, pour out your heart honestly to the Lord and follow His counsel. If you need help in resolving painful memories, seek it now.

You might understandably be concerned about the possible emotional and physical weariness that lies ahead, but you don't face this task alone. In Isaiah, God promises strength to the weary.[5] Daily replenishing power is available. It comes through asking the Lord to meet your need, whether it's a fresh dose of compassion, strength to persevere, or power to forgive. Expectant faith doesn't go unrewarded. In fact, God promises that "those who hope (have confident faith) in the Lord *will* renew their strength."

If you have felt your spiritual life fizzling in recent years, could this ongoing need for God's help be one of His "mysterious ways" to draw you close once again? Coming to Him day in and day out with your inability to cope will inevitably bring you a fresh awareness of His presence and power.

God doesn't want you to merely survive during this season of your life. He wants you to experience His reality—that He does answer prayer, that He is able to do more than all you could ask or imagine, that His ways are not your ways nor His thoughts your thoughts.[6] What is the result God has in mind for your life? That *you* experience His blessing, and that *you* spiritually thrive as you love and serve your mom or dad in His name.

Evaluate Realistically

Will your parents need someone with them around-the-clock? How much time can you give? Who else will be regularly available? Do you have the physical strength to lift them or help with their personal care? Have you had any experience with nursing a sick person?

Another vital area to probe is whether you have the psychological strength needed to care for your parent, particularly if they have Alzheimer's disease. This condition afflicts about 10 percent of those older than sixty-five and nearly 50 percent of those older than eighty-five, leaving them confused, disoriented, and dangerously forgetful.

Patricia Rushford, in her informative work *The Help, Hope, and Cope Book for People with Aging Parents* calls Alzheimer's "the disease of the century."[7] Seventy percent of those with this affliction live with their families. Could you cope with changing diapers, physically restraining your parent, or receiving verbal abuse despite your best efforts?

Plan to Get Help

Some care-givers refuse to let others give them regular respite time. Often it is an attitude of "I can do it" or embarrassment at exposing the condition of their parent to someone other than family that causes this major mistake. Taking either course could destroy you, jeopardize other equally important family relationships, as well as tax yourself unnecessarily.

To prevent this kind of damage from occurring, plan ways to nurture yourself. Give a sympathetic husband a chance to be your helper. Don't go it alone unless you absolutely have to. Be sure to carve out regular times for de-stressing activities.

Consider Care Facilities[8]

"Putting your mom or dad in a nursing home sounds so callous," said Jane, her voice breaking. "I felt like I was signing Mom in to an animal shelter where she'd wait to die."

In spite of a sincere desire to take personal care of her mother, Jane felt she had no choice but to look into a care facility. "Mom was no longer able to get around our apartment by herself. She needed someone to help her to the bathroom and bring her meals during the day," she explained. "As a single, working woman I have no one to watch over her while I'm at the office."

Dabbing at tears, Jane continued, "I know the nursing home is the safest place for Mom right now. They're equipped to give her the medical care and supervision she needs. But I feel so guilty doing this. I feel I have deserted her when she needs me the most."

Jane is not alone in her feelings of guilt for putting a parent in a care facility. But are these guilty feelings valid? Are care facilities really a dumping ground or are they an acceptable alternative? Does recognizing that you cannot meet all your parents' needs at this stage of their life make you a terrible person?

If the day comes when your parent can no longer live in their own home among familiar things, perhaps a multi-level continuing-care facility would be the next best option. Look for one that offers independent living combined with minimal supervision, but is equipped for various levels of dependence as health fails. Far from being horror-houses, these well-managed communities provide outings, companionship, nutritious meals, and even exercise periods designed to produce optimum health. Finding the right facility, however, is a serious venture. For helpful information on what to look for and questions to ask, call your local hospital or state Department of Aging.

When you have done all you can do for your mom or dad, don't let the Accuser rob you of peace regarding the decisions you have made. For your parents' own well-being, help them stay in their home for as long as possible. Failing that, discuss with them what options they have. If this is no longer feasible, you and your family must make the best decision for them and for yourselves. With your thoughts and decisions directed through prayer and God-given wisdom, you can act lovingly and respectfully toward your parents and feel at peace within yourself.

In mid-life it is often our spouse, our children, and our parents who weigh heavily on our minds. But let's turn our attention now toward our own growth and future direction. We'll start by discovering how to move into the future without tripping over the past.

7

If Only I Had . . . or Hadn't

As I savored the last bite of a mega-size slice of chocolate fudge brownie pie, a voice inside started whining, *Oh, if only . . . if only I hadn't eaten the whole thing*!

On another occasion, thinking back on the day as I crawled into bed, I heard that refrain again, *If only . . . if only I hadn't acted like that . . . if only I were perfect.*

I particularly remember one evening when certain members of my family were seated at the dining table ready to eat dinner. As I darted around the kitchen, they began passing the bowls of food. One asked me to bring the ketchup while I was up, and another wanted me to turn down the volume on the stereo.

Without warning, a voice I hardly recognized as my own barked out, "Why can't you do it yourself? I want to sit down and eat!" Heads shot up. Every eye locked on me. "Well," I huffed defensively, "you *could* get up yourselves, instead of asking me to do everything."

So much for being perfect.

"If onlys" come in forms ranging from fleeting remorse to heartbreaking sorrow. Looking at yourself in a full-length mirror might trigger regrets like: *WHY didn't I take off twenty pounds years ago when my body did what it was told?* And even that trauma is nothing compared to living with the painful consequences of more significant choices.

With my own list of "what I'd do differently" tattooed on my conscience, I raised the subject with four friends. Talking with each one privately, I asked what they'd change in their past if they could. Here's what they shared:

Pam, a mother of four, stares at the ashes of family life as she once knew it. Her older son heaps blame on her for the breakup of their home, her older daughter blames their father. The two younger children ricochet emotionally and physically between both parents.

"If only I had understood how to make a relationship work," she lamented. "I was filled with resentment against my husband, Bill. So I insulted him, demeaned him, and used the kids against him. Eventually the hostility between us blew our marriage apart."

Callie, forty-three years old, is married and has three children. She needs to find work to help pay the bills. "Every job that appeals to me requires a degree," she said, frustration in her voice. "If only I had finished school and not jumped at the first opportunity to get married."

Sadness cast a shadow over Nancy's pretty features as she reminisced about her grandmother. "My mother was placed in a mental hospital when I was quite young," she said softly. "Grandma raised me and my sisters, and I loved her dearly. I feel horrible that when she was old and lonely, I was too busy with my life to spend much time with her. If only ... if I could do it again, I'd do things differently."

"I blame myself to this day that I didn't do something more," said Marsha. Now in her forties, Marsha vividly recalls the horror of her younger sister's disappearance twenty years before. "Mary literally disappeared into nowhere. The police looked for her, but after a few weeks my parents gave up all efforts; their grief just immobilized them."

Pain and guilt wrack Marsha whenever she remembers how quickly she and the rest of her family gave up trying to trace Mary. Fueling her anguish is a silent, smouldering rage against her parents for their lack of response to the tragedy.

Mid-life Baggage

If Only I Hadn't ...

Does anyone reach mid-life without regrets? Probably not. Who hasn't struck their child in churning fury, or fantasized about a man other than their spouse? Who hasn't neglected a relationship, or used words or silence to deliberately wound another? Who hasn't wished they could return to the past and change some of the choices that still shape their lives today?

The issue isn't whether or not we have regrets. Each of us can no doubt think of various things we would do differently. The issue is, what have these regrets done to us? How have we handled them? What do we do now?

The Power of Regrets

The four women who shared their mid-life regrets with me were feeling frustration, guilt, sorrow, or anger because of irreversible decisions made earlier in their lives.

Another friend, Cora, had let regrets devour her ability to cope. Hospitalized for severe depression, she tried to commit suicide within days of being admitted. Then, while under the care of a sensitive counselor, she began to examine what she was telling herself about the past and how she responded to these distorted messages. The results surprised her.

"I learned that I was sentencing myself to a lifetime of extreme sadness, tormenting guilt, and utter hopelessness unless I learned to deal with the many regrets in my past," she said. "I fed myself nonstop hate messages because I felt I had failed in every area of my life.

"I was sure other people would hate me too if they knew what I was like, so I didn't let anyone know me beyond a surface relationship. In the end, my view of myself, the people who love me, and especially God was totally warped and twisted."

Now, two years after her hospitalization, Cora marvels at the change in her thinking and self-perception. "To go from cowering in the corner of a padded isolation room in the psychiatric unit to laughing and enjoying life is a miracle," she said with a huge smile. "I feel free of the emotional chains that I dragged around every day for years. Truly accepting that I am forgiven, that I am not a horrible person, but God's precious child, has liberated my whole outlook on life."

What effect do the "if onlys" from your past have on you today? Do they flit through your mind once in a while, or do they assault your conscience on a daily basis?

If Only They Hadn't . . .

In mid-life it's easy to recall our own poor choices in the past. But at times we also hold tightly to the pain others have inflicted on us.

How would you finish the phrase "If only he hadn't . . . ," or, "If only she hadn't . . ."? What flashes into your mind? Huddling in fear after being abused? Shrinking from verbal assault by someone you loved? Enduring false accusations that shredded your reputation and ability to trust? Staring in disbelief as your husband tells you he's leaving? Sadly, the list goes on because life is rarely tidy, pain-free, or picture-perfect.

Much as we would like to think it possible, it's naïve to imagine we can walk in this world without experiencing some degree of pain or injustice. In his sensitive and helpful book *Healing for Damaged Emotions*,[1] Dr. David Seamands states, "Today many Christians struggle with emotional pain that is deeply rooted in the past."

Wounding can happen in childhood or in adult years. No matter when the hurt occurred, learning to acknowledge it is the first step toward emotional wellness. Too often, though, in order to cope, pain is pushed under the surface.

But denying pain doesn't make it go away. The healing process can only begin when buried pain is exposed and dealt with.

Emotional damage we thought we had dealt with in the past announces its presence through overly hostile feelings, an envious or critical spirit, depression, and feelings of guilt, shame, and worthlessness. Frequently these signs, recognized by others, are invisible to us.

How can you determine if past regrets or pain inflicted by others are affecting you today? Try taking your emotional pulse by asking yourself these questions:

Would I characterize myself as drained by feelings of un-worthiness, failure, guilt, or anger? Or am I energized by love, joy, peace, and the other fruits of the Spirit?[2]

Do I struggle with bitterness because of mistreatment in my past, or have I faced up to and broken the emotional grip those events have had on my life?

Am I angry with God because He allowed me to suffer, or do I see and believe that He is weaving all things together for my good?

If you want to move into the next half of your life emo-tionally healthy, you must honestly address your own per-sonal collection of "if onlys." In writing to the Philippian believers, the apostle Paul described how he dealt with his past. "One thing I do," he said, "forgetting what is behind and straining toward what is ahead, I press on toward the goal."[3]

Saul (who became Paul) hated and persecuted the early Christians. He could have chosen to let what he did trap him in guilt and regret. Instead, after he encountered the risen Christ, he threw off past baggage and made a choice: deal with what happened, forget it, and press on, rejoicing in His Lord's forgiveness.

As women in the middle years, we need to follow Paul's example and choose to move on from the hurts and losses experienced in life. This is not an easy or quick process. There is no one-size-fits-all time line. But there are some one-size-fits-all steps to take if we want to say goodbye to past hurts.

In these middle years we face a decision between looking at the negative events in our lives and moving on or staying stuck in blame and guilt. All through life we make choices, and those choices have formed who we are today. In the same way, our choices from today forward make us who we will become. A challenging couplet goes: "Two men looked through prison bars, one saw mud, the other stars." Like those two men, you and I can make choices. We can't erase wrongs done to us or wrongs we have done, but we can control how those events affect us. What we need to do is look back and let go.

Looking Back

Grappling with painful memories is as much fun as having the dentist approach you with a six-inch needle. He promises to take away the pain shooting through your cracked tooth. But you have to get past that needle first. . . . It makes you shudder. Much as you hate the process, his promise turns out to be true. Likewise, if you have hidden from the past, looking back at the ugly things done to you, and that you have done, can be painful.

Several years ago, staring at my face in the mirror, I made a profound observation: *This is the best it will ever be.* I now avoid looking in mirrors except when absolutely necessary.

To look back is to gaze into another kind of mirror, one that is too important to avoid. This mirror is your heart. And, what you see in this mirror CAN be changed for the better.

Healing Begins With Honesty

My friend Pam spent several years hiding behind walls of blame after her divorce. This is a common response to loss. In pain we lash out like wounded animals, determined that someone be held responsible for our suffering. We rage against the other person, attack ourselves, even shake our fist at God (surely *He* could have prevented everything).

To erase the regrets and bitterness that bombarded her, Pam came to realize she had to change her response to what had happened. Can you identify with her candid description of the emotions and thoughts that filled her heart?

My stomach churned with fury every day when I thought of Bill. He was an angry, selfish, abusive man, and he continued acting that way after the divorce.

The more I struggled with changes in my circumstances—moving from a comfortable home to a small apartment, the more I blamed him. I hated him for forcing me to give up being a homemaker after nearly thirty years, and become a single, working mom. As far as I was concerned, Bill deserved the blame for everything.

As the bitter effects of Pam and Bill's divorce affected their four children, the family split into factions—"I'm on Mom's side" or "I'm on Dad's side." In addition to scathing comments from her ex-husband about her failures as a wife and mother, Pam found herself the target of bitter words from some of her children.

> For a long time, I could only see Bill's faults. But after being pounded by criticism from others in my family, I began to blame myself for everything. I told myself I had been a horrible mother. I had nagged. I was mean and demanding. I had been cold to Bill.
>
> At that point, I added feelings of worthlessness and guilt to the emotional fury and self-pity boiling inside me.

Staggering under the emotional strain of a major life crisis and transition, plus the rejection and hostility of family members, Pam's blame flared in another direction. Why didn't the One who could do the impossible prevent all this mess from happening?

> In addition to thinking *if only Bill hadn't* ... and *if only I hadn't* ..., I found myself angrily saying, "God, If only *you* hadn't ..." Why did He allow us to go on like this and end up with such pain and brokenness? Why hadn't He kept our family together?
>
> So at this point I added another ingredient to my emotional stew: anger toward God.

It's easy to pick out the messages Pam was stuffing down every day: hatred for Bill, contempt for herself, and cynicism toward God. The result was that she remained stuck in a deadly cycle of depression, tears, and hopelessness.

What images from the past do you mentally chew on? Have you dealt with the feelings those images arouse, or have you refused to acknowledge their existence? Learning to let go of negative feelings is essential if we want to move into the next half of life without tripping over the past. Happily, Pam didn't remain stuck. She decided to switch her gaze from mud to stars. Following are some of the steps she took to shed the past and move forward.

Let Go

Step One: Reject Blame and Bitterness

The tapes run in an endless loop: *It's all your fault. You ruined my life. I wouldn't be suffering like this if only you hadn't . . .* Blaming others is exhausting and it gets us nowhere—like a hampster running on a wheel.

You may have been terribly mistreated by another person. It is understandable to be angry at their sin against you. It is also true that not everything that happens in life is your fault. If your emotional pain is rooted in childhood mistreatment, you are certainly not to blame for what happened. Yet to cling to the anger you feel is a choice you make yourself.

Blaming others for our suffering keeps alive a victim mentality that cripples growth. When we play this blame game we trap ourselves in the past. Nothing changes. And think about it: the other person isn't affected by our bitterness. But *we* are. Holding on to negative feelings delays *our* own healing.

Joseph spent thirteen years suffering the painful consequences of his brothers' hatred (Genesis 37–50). But when his brothers were within his power to punish, he fully forgave them.

"You intended to harm me," he said to them. Then, revealing his insight into God's purposes, he concluded, "but God intended it for good."[4]

Joseph was confident of three truths:

1. God does not abandon His own. God was with him in every unfair experience he encountered. Not to punish, not to rejoice over his pain, but to give strength and comfort.
2. God uses trials to transform us. Joseph understood that God allowed his bitter experiences and that He used them as preparation for future service.
3. God incorporates our suffering into His plans. God mysteriously wove His plans to bless Joseph, and the descendants of Abraham, in and through his years of suffering.

It has been said that life is 10 percent what happens to us and 90 percent how we react to it. When our response is to cry out to God for help to overcome evil with good, be free of hatred, and receive His power to forgive, we profit and grow through the harm done to us.[5] The mental chains that anchor us to the past can be thrown off, but it requires of us a willingness to forgive those who caused our pain.

Step Two: Forgive the Offender

Forgiveness has been described as love's toughest work. If you've been deeply wounded and struggle with forgiving, you probably agree with that description.

What is forgiveness? It is not minimizing or excusing the sin of another. It is choosing to surrender your right to get even, to make the other pay, to seek revenge. Forgiveness is the willingness to absorb the pain and suffering that someone's failures and sins have caused you.

Why forgive? Because God has forgiven our many offenses and commands that we forgive others. Forgiveness reflects the character of Jesus, who forgave while he suffered on the cross. For our own emotional, physical, and spiritual wholeness we need to forgive.

How do we forgive? First, pray for willingness to forgive. It is a process, not a quick decision. Here are some steps suggested by Beverly Flanagan in her book *Forgiving the Unforgivable*.

Name the injury—what were the losses you experienced?
Claim the injury—what were its effects on you?
Blame the injurer—yes, he/she hurt you. Acknowledge it.
Balance the scales—how can you grow from that offense?
Choose to forgive—you are responsible for your attitude.
Establish a new identity that is not tied to past hurts.

Forgiveness doesn't mean "I trust you." Joseph didn't trust his brothers when they first appeared in Egypt. Nor does forgiveness mean everything is as it was, or that there are no consequences. Nevertheless, whether or not the relationship is restored, forgiving your offender releases you from being an emotional captive. And that is vital for healing.

Often, seeking help from a mature friend, pastor, or counselor is the key to shaking off the past. Don't let pain and hurt rob you of all God has for you. Take action.

Pam's journey toward wholeness began by forgiving Bill for the suffering he caused her. Later, she was able to ask his forgiveness for her part in the destruction of their family. Letting go of her bitterness meant acknowledging she had the power to choose her attitudes, thoughts, and behavior. This enabled her to stop living in the past and to stop nursing her wounds and harboring blame. She chose, instead, to take responsibility for her feelings, begin the healing process, and move on.

Step Three: Discern Between Real and False Guilt

Listen to your own self-talk. *What do you hear? I am to blame. I am a bad person. No one I know would ever react the way I did. I am worse than others. I deserve all that's happened. I should have ... I could have ... I ought to have ...*

Playing the blame game with yourself as the major culprit is like clubbing yourself on the head with a baseball bat. You'll have little to show for it besides a headache. Yes, you may have failed. But failure isn't unique to you. The rest of the human race has failed as well.

God made us with the capacity to feel guilt. But we must discern between real and false guilt. There are ways to identify godly guilt:

Be Open to Conviction. Ask God to search your heart. When wrong attitudes, acts, or bitter words come to mind, write them down without excusing yourself.

Confess. Acknowledge the sin in your own heart, and confess what those sins are. Name them before God, taking comfort in the fact that He knows better than we do that we are marred by sin.

Repent. Acknowledge that you are truly sorry for your wrong behavior. Tell God you want to turn around and go in a different direction with your life.

Ask for Forgiveness. Although we are all without excuse in God's eyes, He is compassionate, knowing we are like dust, weak, and in great need of forgiveness and cleansing.[6] You can claim His forgiveness and reject false guilt, along with its shroud of condemnation. God has set you free. Go forward in peace.

After taking these three steps toward inner healing, Pam moved forward on her journey to emotional wholeness. One more step remained to be taken.

Step Four: Get to Know God Better

Have you ever found yourself thinking: If God really cared, why did He allow this to happen? Why didn't God step in and do something? I thought He could do anything.

When some experience sends you reeling, do you rage at God? Do you question His love or goodness or power?

Our natural desire is for life to be full of comfort, ease, and pleasure. In fact, one of my favorite "oldie but goldie" hymns asks the question: "Shall I be carried to the skies on flowery beds of ease?" I always want to shout, "YES!" That's just how I'd like my life to be—no pain, no thorns, no suffering. Don't you agree? Unfortunately, God doesn't usually let us go through life like this. In fact, He makes it clear that He uses hard circumstances to mold and mature us.

Does God care? Does he care about us even though life hurts? *Yes*. Does he wave a magic wand and take the pain away? *No*. What he does promise is to:

give strength to overcome the temptation to be bitter or filled with self-pity;

provide us with a guidebook (his Word) to healthy human behavior and relationships;

assure us in his Word of our worth and value as women made in his image and belonging to him;

send his Spirit to live in us;

give us the power to actually do what he says when we're sure we can't;

be available when we need help NOW.

Believing that God is indifferent to our disappointments, grief, or struggles is a lie of the Enemy. God doesn't sit with his arms folded, wondering why we're crying over the past. Through his Word, the gentle drawing of the Holy Spirit, the invitation of Jesus, and the love of fellow believers, he longs to remind us that he is the great Burden-Bearer, the Comforter. He is the One who can do far beyond all we ask or imagine. He is the All-Wise God, whose plans are to prosper us, not to bring us harm; to give us a hope and a future.[7]

When Pam saw how anger and self-pity had blinded her to God's tender care, she wept. Her "if onlys" had proven to be tools of bondage keeping her distanced from God, bitter, and focused on the past. Actively choosing to move toward healing and a more intimate relationship with God, Pam found the power of her "if onlys" to keep her living in the past was broken.

What will you do with your "if onlys"?

To finish well is more important than to start well, so let's keep moving forward. Having considered how to get rid of our emotional baggage, let's tackle those nagging thoughts of *I can't do that . . . or can I?*

8

I Can't Do That . . .
or Can I?

"Do you want to go whitewater rafting on the Rogue River?" asked Jim. "A group of friends from work is going and they've invited us to join them."

"That sounds great," I responded, my mind filling with pictures of us floating lazily down the river under a scorching sun, the gentle spray cooling our hot, relaxed bodies. Not being the camping sort, however, one thought disturbed me. "Jim," I asked cautiously, "will there be indoor plumbing at the campsites along the river?" One look at the amused smile on his face, and I knew the answer.

The trip began just as I had imagined. The sun burned hot, spray blew in our faces, and the oarsmen rowed quietly. A blissful experience. As hawks drifted overhead and the stillness of the forest embraced us like a soft blanket, my disturbed thoughts of living without the comforts of civilization slipped away.

The raft Jim and I were assigned to was loaded with heavy boxes tightly lashed to the frame and filling up a third of the space. They contained the group's supplies for our three-day trip. To keep up his strength, our oarsman, a wiry, middle-aged man, took frequent sips from a bottle wedged into a small space beside him. I never did find out what was in the bottle, but I doubt that it was sparkling water.

Before too long, a dull roar broke through the silence.

"What's that?" I asked, trying to sound nonchalant. "The first rapids," Jim replied excitedly. "Now the fun begins."

In a matter of minutes, the raft began to buck like an unbroken colt. Leaping high in the air, crashing down, bending in half and lurching forward, we rushed headlong into the first set of rapids. With split-second timing our oarsman expertly maneuvered the raft between rocks. Then, without warning, we slammed into a huge boulder the size of an army tank. As we turned around to see if the other rafts were safe, the one behind hit us at full force, jamming us farther up onto the rock.

"We're stuck!" shouted the oarsman above the roar of the rapids. "You'll all have to get out." Stumbling and slipping, I obeyed, climbed up to a flat area and looked out over the churning river. The worst of the rapids were behind us, but now we were marooned in the middle of an endless stream of rushing water.

"How are we going to get off?" I asked Jim, my voice trembling. I didn't have to wait long for the answer. Shouting at the five of us huddled on the rock, the oarsman said, "We can't let you get back in the rafts. We won't be able to pull them off the rocks. You'll all have to swim to shore. Get down by the edge, lean back and let the current take you downstream. Your lifejackets will keep you afloat."

Having inherited my mother's lack of courage, I immediately panicked. "Jim, I can't swim to shore, I'll drown," I cried. "I hate the water. Why didn't anyone tell me this could happen? Can't they send in a helicopter to winch us off this rock? Surely somebody can rescue us."

Firmly, my stoic husband informed me, "No one knows we're stuck on this rock. No helicopter is going to rescue you. You have two choices: Stay here on the rock or swim off like the rest of us." Then, tenderly wrapping his arms around me, he added, "Don't worry. You can do it."

If you're going to thrive in mid-life, you have to do battle with your fears, climb off your rock, and immerse yourself in the river of growth. Like swirling down the Rogue River minus a raft, saying *yes* to new experiences can appear very frightening. But not to expand the horizons of your experience at mid-life is to risk stagnating and closing in on yourself. With the other half of your adult life ahead of you, you're too young to bury your abilities, give up your dreams, or settle in a rut.

In her bestseller *New Passages: Mapping Your Life Across Time*,[1] Gail Sheehy discusses today's increasing life-span. What does it mean for those of us in the middle years? Are we "over the hill" once we're past forty? No. Her research suggests we are entering vast new territories of second adulthood.

She says, "Ahead of us lie years filled with opportunities for development, growth, and mastery."

Let's build on that by asking ourselves how God wants us, the first generation of women to live so long, to fill these extra years. How about further development and use of the talents and gifts He has given? Or looking for those good works He's planned for you to do? Eliminate from your vocabulary the excuse, "I can't do that, I'm too old." Hold on, instead, to Christ's promise of abundant, fulfilling life to those who live for Him. His promises don't come with a time limit attached.[2]

So what's needed to get the maximum out of these midlife years that brim with promise? The first step is to begin examining your thinking, because the decision to expand or contract the walls of your life begins in your mind. It's what we think and focus on that causes us to say yes or no to God and the opportunities for growth He brings. Like prison doors that clang shut automatically, feelings of fear, intimidation, inadequacy, and lack of faith can keep us locked up, unable to move forward. Self-sabotaging thoughts close off any willingness to trust God and to risk. The result is an all too familiar one. When facing new challenges we respond with the frightened cry, "I can't do that!"

Is it possible to move beyond these common fears, even if you've spent many years wrestling with them? Yes. Growth *can* happen. You *can* overcome your tendency to shrink back. You *can* find the courage to step off the rock, to let God's current take you downstream to new adventures in your life.

Here's a simple acrostic that can clarify your thinking and help you say yes to all God has ahead for you.

G Guard Your Mind

R Review Your Self-Talk

O Observe Your Emotions/Feelings

W Weigh Your Choices

T Think the Truth

H Hear and Act

Guard Your Mind

Examine Your Stereotypes

In mid-life, we have to guard our minds, thinking carefully about what we tell ourselves. Do you allow outdated stereotypes to sneak in? Examine and discard them, because they have power to undermine your future direction.

If we believe the adage "You can't teach an old dog new tricks," we'll shrink from challenging ourselves to learn. If we think being middle-aged means coddling ourselves physically, we'll never try new activities. And if we feel our lives are set in rigid, unbreakable molds, we'll allow boredom to sap the vitality that comes from fresh input and experiences.

The key to releasing ourselves from a self-imposed cage is to shake off limiting stereotypes that flash before us like warning signals: *Mid-life means decline; my mind is too set to learn anything new; my choices are limited. . . .*

Once we dump these dreary stereotypes, we'll see some of the most exciting and fulfilling years of our lives stretching out before us. Not only can these years be filled with personal growth, they can also encourage, teach, and model to other women what it means to be a mature Christian woman who wants her life to count for God.

Listen to Yourself!

Do you talk to yourself? I really enjoy chatting away in my head. Wheeling my cart through the grocery store, I have vigorous internal discussions. *Look at that,* I say to myself, *cereal has gone up again! I'm not paying those prices.* In response, another voice says, *Well, you have to. That's the only kind the kids will eat.* These conversations make shopping a stimulating event. The only time they cause me any trouble is when I get overexcited and start talking out loud.

I also talk to myself when baking. And driving. And then there are the times when I stand at the open door of the fridge and ask, *Was I looking for something or putting something away?*

Are we crazy because we talk to ourselves? Is it a mid-life affliction? No, we all talk to ourselves. But what we say may not always be true.

When God shows you a need, or opens a door to a job opportunity or a new venture, what is your reaction? "Oh, I can't do that." Or, "Maybe I can. Yes, I'll give it a try." Are you prompted by fear or by faith that if God wants you to do something, He'll make you able? Your response depends on what you tell yourself.

Scripture spotlights the powerful role our minds play in the issues of life. Being aware of what you're thinking and telling yourself is not only pivotal but vital. In fact, your future fulfillment and direction depend on it.

Review Your Self-Talk

Watch for Negative Messages

Some people are naturally optimistic. They feed their minds positive messages and rarely battle negative self-talk. My friend Carol is one of these upbeat people. Determined to achieve her dream of becoming a child therapist, she recently returned to college to complete her degree. "I love new challenges," she said. "I didn't hesitate about going back to school because I usually feel confident and capable when I take on new tasks."

If you find it hard to identify with Carol, you're not alone. Negative self-talk has many causes. Let's identify three of them.

Self-Assessment

When God first appeared to Moses in the burning bush and called him to lead the Israelites out of bondage, Moses' response was, "I can't do that."

The ten spies sent into the Promised Land forgot God's assurances of victory, looked only at their puny personal resources and said in unison, "We can't do that." (Numbers 13).

Many years later, Jeremiah added another dimension to the same response. Feeling overwhelmed and completely inadequate, he declared, "I can't do that, I am only a child."[3] As women past our youthful years, this is one excuse we can't legitimately use. Nevertheless, our negative self-assessment can prompt us to react in the same way.

Spiritual Attack

The apostle Peter warns us to watch for attack from an unseen source. He writes, "Be self-controlled and alert." He knew all too well that we have an enemy, the devil, who prowls around like a roaring lion looking for someone to devour.[4] The devil is not a little fellow with a red suit and a pitchfork, but a powerful opponent who seeks to confuse our thinking, turn our emotions against our own best interests, and misguide our choices. He plants doubts, fear, intimidation, and tries to get us to focus on ourselves rather than on God's provision.

Skewed Interpretation of Events

What do you tell yourself when you've had an uncomfortable experience? Look at the following distortions. Do any of them have a familiar ring?

Overgeneralization: You see a single negative event as a pattern. You tell yourself, "If it happened once, it'll happen again."

All-or-Nothing Thinking: Everything is black or white. You tell yourself, "I can never do anything right. I'm a failure."

Mental Filter: You dwell on one negative detail and filter out all that is positive. You tell yourself, "If I was really capable, that wouldn't have happened."

Jumping to Conclusions: You make a negative interpretation. Convinced you're right, you don't attempt to check out the facts. You tell yourself, "I know that's how people look at me."

Emotional Reasoning: You assume that because you feel something it must be true. You tell yourself, "If it weren't true, I wouldn't feel this way."[5]

Whether our negative self-talk and misbeliefs come from our own insecurities, the Enemy, or distorted interpretations, we must take charge of these internal messages. Are you wondering if what you think or how you interpret experiences really matters? Yes, it does. What you tell yourself is more important than you might realize.[6]

Eliminate Self-Sabotaging Statements

Both Moses and Jeremiah believed certain things about themselves. Their distorted views of who they were and what they were capable of would have continued if God had not stepped in and challenged their thinking. To free yourself from similar self-sabotaging statements, ask God to help you monitor your thoughts. You might also ask a friend to point out any negative statements they hear you make about yourself.

Linda was so determined to put a stop to verbally running herself down that she asked her good friend Molly for help. Whenever Molly heard one of Linda's slams against herself, she burst out with "Liar, liar, pants on fire!" With Molly's aid, Linda saw how she was reinforcing her own poor self-image and allowing Satan to defeat and discourage her through her self-talk. Now, when she catches herself saying negative or fearful things in her mind, she chants under her breath, "Liar, liar, pants on fire!"

What are some self-sabotaging statements that can trip us up? Are any of these familiar to you?

Putting yourself down. You think, *How can they believe I'm the right person for this position? I'm not smart enough. I don't know how to. . . .*

Anticipating failure. You tell yourself, *I'm inadequate. I know I'll fail. I'll look foolish for having tried and everyone will laugh.*

Fearing what people think. You're awash in unnerving thoughts like *I want everyone to think well of me so I must look and act in ways that will gain their approval. If they disapprove of me, I'll feel awful.*

Blaming others. Your mind runs amok with *If it wasn't for my (husband, family, finances, lack of skills . . .), I could do that.*

To detect your own defeatist messages, pull up your thoughts and study them for accuracy and logic. Question and probe. "Am I telling myself the truth or not?" Developing a constant awareness of your inner talk takes time, but don't let up. As with any worthwhile habit, you'll benefit enormously in the long run.

Observe Your Emotions/Feelings

Negative self-talk triggers a downward emotional spiral. David the psalmist knew this and modeled what we need to do. He questioned his feelings by asking, "Why are you downcast, O my soul? Why so disturbed within me?"[7] David paid attention to his emotions, recognizing they were a clue to his self-talk.

If we're going to enter the river of growth we need to follow David's example, realizing our emotions often reflect what we're thinking. This is especially true of feelings that cause us to cling to our familiar rock, refusing to risk. What powerful emotions do we need to identify in ourselves?

Anxiety, Worry, Concern: These are fed by thinking, *It would be awful, terrible, humiliating if I failed a test, or didn't get the job.*

Depression, discouragement: We aggravate these by thinking, *Why try? I can't do it. My energy's gone. It's too late to start again.*

Fear is fed by thinking, *Don't risk. Stay with what's familiar and comfortable. Protect yourself from the unknown.*

Defeat is heightened by saying, *Other women are more capable than I am. I can't measure up.*

Indecision grows from thoughts such as, *I don't know what to do. Maybe it's better to do nothing than to do the wrong thing.*

When you allow unexamined emotions to motivate and control your responses, you give them power over your future. If you feel pressured by negative feelings to make a particular decision, recognize this as a signal to stop and probe what you're telling yourself. Cultivate the habit of examining your emotions by putting them under the microscope of truth. Here are some ways you can do this:

Label your feelings. State: *I feel* _____ *when I* _____ *consider.*

Look behind your feelings. Ask: *What am I telling myself that is producing these feelings?*

Question your assumptions. Probe: *Is what I'm telling myself true? How do I know?*

Invite God into the picture. Pray: *Lord, is my future written in stone or could my assumptions be wrong? Have I taken into account Your power to work in me and my circumstances?*

Reassess your feelings. Evaluate: *Are fears, wrong assumptions, or lack of faith behind my feelings? What would happen if truth and trust in God replaced my distorted self-talk?*

God wants you to experience positive, joyful emotions—not fear, insecurity, and defeat. This is possible if you learn to check your self-talk and observe the feelings these thoughts stir up. When you've done this, you're ready for the next step toward G.R.O.W.T.H.

Weigh Your Choices

Standing on a rock in the middle of the rapids, I had no choice. I had to let the river carry me along, and I prayed I'd survive the ride of my life. But deciding to jump into the river of growth that swirls through mid-life is a choice. We can stand on our rock and insist, "I'm not going anywhere," or we can say, "I'm frightened by the unknown but I'm not going to let my feelings hold me back."

We face choices throughout life. We have made choices in the past regarding our education, marriage, career, and personal pursuits. Not only did we choose what we wanted to do, we also made choices along the way that have made us the kind of person we are today.

Our attitudes toward our abilities, circumstances, and options in life are formed by us alone. We decide on our mindset regarding the past, we decide how we think in the present, and we decide how we'll view the future.

Our choices not only determine the course of our lives, they affect the lives of others, too. They also reveal our values, priorities, and spiritual maturity.

We constantly make choices, even without realizing it. We choose to:

Say, "I can't do that," *or*, "I can do all things through Christ who strengthens me."

Search out creative solutions *or* fatalistically believe we're locked into the status quo.

Declare, "It'll never work," *or*, "I'll give it a try."

Have faith and hope *or* be worried and despairing.

Praise God *or* pity ourselves.

Listen to demoralizing self-talk *or* focus on biblical truths that spur us on to growth.

God has given us the privilege and responsibility of making life-changing choices. In the years leading up to mid-life, we've made so many choices it's impossible to remember them all. But if we take a clear look at our life and our character, what we see is to a large extent the result of all those choices.

Knowing this, think about the choices you make today. What effect will they have on your life ten or twenty years from now? Will the choices you make today produce what matters tomorrow?

Our choices do more than help us survive, they provide the basis for thriving in mid-life and beyond.

Think the Truth

Before the truth of who we are in God's eyes can come alive, ignite confidence, and give us courage to act, we must believe it. Before we can believe it, however, we need to know what God says about his own.

God's View of You

Do you believe you are precious to God? Do you know in your heart—not just your head—that you are loved, liked, valued, and approved of by the God of the universe? Can you grasp the empowering principle that God doesn't call you to do anything he won't equip you to do? These are truths he wants you to depend on.

A Christian since her teens, Brenda had a deep love for God, but she found it hard to truly feel that he loved her. "I wanted to go beyond *knowing* God loves me," she said, "I wanted to *feel* loved. After praying to him about my longing, I decided to start reprogramming my mind with truth from the Bible. I did this by picturing myself standing under a warm shower flowing with God's love and affirmation. Then I'd repeat to myself words and phrases that God uses in his Word to describe his children. I'd do this over and over, whenever I found negative tapes running through my mind."[8]

By renewing her mind with truth taken directly from Scripture, Brenda began to walk in a conscious awareness of God's love. "Learning to tell myself the truth changed my relationship with God," she recounted with delight. "I still get a little scared when I face new situations, but I thank God for his caring love, remind myself that he wants me to succeed, and remember that I am not alone in any situation. Holding on to these facts has helped me kick the 'I can't do that' syndrome."

Your View of Yourself

Thinking the truth means breaking the habit of beating yourself down. Do you believe your heavenly father has a negative view of you? Can you imagine him attacking you with the destructive, demeaning words that you heap on yourself? Would you say what you say to yourself to a friend or someone else you love?

Tearing yourself down is not only a misery-producing habit, it dishonors the One who created you and is at work in your life. Breaking the hold of lifelong thinking patterns takes time, but it can be done. To think accurately about yourself, yank out those weeds that have no basis in truth. In their place, start seeding your mind with biblically sound statements.

You might want to begin the process of renewing your mind by praying truth: "Father, you have told me I am unique. You have given me gifts and abilities. You and I know I'm not perfect, but I thank you for loving me despite my failings. Lord, you don't measure me against my sister, my mother, or anyone else. Since you, Lord, have assured me that I am not a helpless victim of my circumstances, I know I can change. By your power, I am able to accomplish whatever you desire me to do. Amen and amen."

Seize these truths, search the Scriptures for more, write them down, chew them over, and verbalize them in intimate conversations with God. Do this, and the powerful grip negative self-talk has over you will be broken.

Hear and Act

One description of insanity is "doing the same thing over and over, expecting things to turn out differently."[9] Only you can determine what needs to change if you want different results in your life. You alone must decide what effort you are willing to make to experience growth.

You might already be paddling along as fast as you want to go in the river of growth. Or maybe you're happily floating along, content, at peace with yourself and God's purposes for you.

But if you find yourself restless, feeling that life is stale, understand that staying in the same patterns will not produce different results. Pay attention to your inner stirrings. God may be getting you ready to take another direction, or preparing you to add another, unimagined, dimension to your life.

When God nudges you to look beyond your present horizons, motivates you to explore new areas of growth, or challenges you to rearrange your priorities, change *will* happen. Releasing your grip on what has been safe and familiar involves taking a risk, but growth only comes when we climb off our rock and plunge into the river. Whether that risk is talking to a new neighbor or applying for law school, it's essential for thriving in the years ahead.

The New Testament writer James urges, "Do not merely listen to the word. . . . Do what it says."[10] As you work through this all-important transition into your "second" adult life-span, pray, listen carefully, act on God's leading, and stomp on those "I can't do that" tapes.

After all, how do you know if you don't try?

Once you've discarded those inner messages that trip you up, the next step to making the most of mid-life is answering the question, "Who am I now that I've grown up?"

9

Who Am I, Now That I've Grown Up?

I'd always wondered who I really was. From my earliest days I pondered darkly, *Am I really from this family or am I adopted? How is it that I'm blonde and my sisters are brunettes? What don't I know?* Despite my parents' tales of my birth on a stormy February night in the Outer Hebrides of Scotland, and their frequent reassurances, I still harbored my suspicions.

Then, twenty-two years later, before women's lib might have rescued me from my dilemma with a hyphenated name, I mulled over my future identity. I had fallen in love with a wonderful man, but could I really face being called "Mrs.

Smith" the rest of my days? I married a Jim Smith, brother to John Smith and Mary Smith. Now, by way of an eager "I do," the stroke of a pen on a marriage certificate, and a shortened version of my given name, I became Pat Smith. And so I remained . . . until I came to mid-life.

"You're calling yourself what?" said my husband in shock. "Oh, mother. Please don't do that," groaned our two children. "Poppy, that's wonderful," beamed my father, who happily phoned the good news around England to my sisters. Poppy, the name they had called me since I was little, had been proudly restored to use.

What prompted this bold yet chaotic change? One day, in the middle of ploughing through mid-life thoughts, I realized I always call myself "Poppy." Whenever I chatted to myself or told myself off, I'd always begin, "Poppy Smith . . ." Besides, I decided, "Poppy" has more zing, more cachet, more . . .

"Sounds more like Popeye to me," muttered my husband, shaking his head in bewilderment at another of his wife's mid-life escapades.

If someone asked you, "Who are you, now that you've grown up?" what would you say? How would you answer that question for yourself? Not surprisingly, the answer changes with the years.

For Joni Eareckson Tada, the answer is something she never dreamed of as a young woman of seventeen. When Joni gave the keynote address at a large conference, I listened intently, captured not only by what she said but also by her spirit. She had clearly accepted what God had allowed to touch her life. Joni took the tragedy of being paralyzed as a challenge, offered herself to God, and became His tool to bring hope and courage to others.

God knew what He wanted to do through Joni's life as she yielded it to Him, but she had no idea what He had in mind for her. The same is true for you and for me as we stand poised on the brink of our second adult life-span.

As women in the middle years, we can look back over several decades and trace God's shaping of our lives. By virtue of being female, we have many experiences in common. Even so, we've each walked a unique path. No one else has lived in my shoes, nor in yours. We've responded in our own ways to times of anxiety, crisis, or blessing. Now, here we are, adult women—the sum of our individual life experiences, the roles we've played, our personalities, and the gifts, talents, and skills we've accumulated.

We've changed, matured, evolved from who we once were. Act Two of our adult lives lies ahead. We move into it not only packaged differently but with different contents.

In our quest to not merely survive but thrive in these middle years and beyond, let's tackle our next task—identifying what makes us who we are. When we know who we are and where we've come from, we'll have an invaluable resource to help us make the best choices in the days ahead.

To kick off the dissecting process, let's begin with some simple self-analysis. As you work through various exercises to discover who you are and where you're going, you'll be accumulating a lot of valuable information worth keeping. Why not record it in a pretty notebook, perhaps one with flowers or stripes or polka-dots—whatever reflects your personality. If you prefer to grab a few sheets of paper or write on the backs of envelopes, go ahead. Carve out some alone time and begin to think about who you really are, now that you've grown up.

I'm a Person Who . . .

Leafing through a travel magazine that specialized in exotic trips, my husband exclaimed, "Wouldn't this be fun!"

Glancing over his shoulder at the photo that had excited his imagination, I gasped, "Jim, you must be crazy. I'm the last person to spend a vacation crouched on the back of an elephant lumbering through the jungles of Thailand." Knowing who you are and who you aren't is essential when married to someone who thrives on the unusual.

Whether glorious or ghastly, vacations are a minor part of life. When you add up all of life's segments, however, knowing yourself and your likes and dislikes becomes vital. At this point in our lives, most of us know if we are basically introverts who keep our thoughts and opinions to ourselves, or extroverts who happily tell everyone whatever they'd like to know about us. Of course, we could be a mix of the two depending on the circumstances. But see if you recognize yourself in any of the following:

Thinker	mulls things over, takes time to answer
Feeler	spontaneous, easily made mad, glad, or sad
Saver	puts as much away as possible for a rainy day
Spender	spends today—a rainy day might never come
Ambler	relaxed, inspects every item in the shop
Scurrier	goal-oriented; hurry, get it done NOW
Opinionated	strong views, dogmatic, must win
Adaptable	easygoing, unruffled, peacemaker[1]

To discover even more about yourself, stop and reflect on the following statements. Answer them as honestly as you can—no one else needs to see what you truly think. As fresh insights come, be sure to write them down.

I enjoy being with people who are . . .

I judge others by _____ because . . .

I put things off when . . .

I enjoy doing _____ with my leisure time.

My appearance matters to me because . . .

I would like to change_____ in my life.

Some goals I've accomplished are . . .

I feel anxious when . . .

Three strengths I have are . . .

Three areas I struggle with are . . .[2]

My Life's Been Shaped By . . .

Tucked away with other treasures from my husband's bachelor days in Kenya, when he was a doctor treating Peace Corps volunteers, are several soapstone candlesticks. Each one is hand-carved from a solid piece of soapstone, and each is unique. Whether tall, elegant pillars or squatty and rounded, their purpose is the same: to shed light in the darkness.

As followers of Jesus Christ, we have the same ultimate purpose—to shed light wherever we are placed. How we do that, however, varies according to the way we've been shaped by the Master Sculptor.

God has been in the life-and-character-shaping business for a very long time. Throughout history, he has put people in place to accomplish His purposes. By shaping and polishing inherited abilities, spiritual sensitivity, and life experiences, God forms a person He can use. When that person chooses to respond in obedience to Him, much is accomplished for God's kingdom. Consider some of the more famous examples of his handiwork:

Joseph: wrenched from his family to become a leader in Egypt.

Moses: trained in leadership while in Pharoah's household and called, instead, to lead the Israelites to freedom.

Esther: blessed with inner and outer beauty that won her a crown and the opportunity to save her people.

Daniel: whose courage, convictions, and gift of prophecy placed him in the circle of court advisers.

Paul: whose tenacious character and brilliant mind became tools God used to spread the gospel.

Barnabas: an encourager, strengthening many in the tumultuous years of the early church.

In weaving your life into strong and sturdy stuff that he can use, God draws on all the various strands that form who you are. Not only has he used your gifts and abilities in the past, he wants to continue to do so today—except now, at mid-life, it's time to make sure that where you invest your time is truly where your strengths and God's purposes mesh together.

Someone has said, "Life is like a coin. You can spend it any way you wish, but you can spend it only once."

How have you spent your life so far? How do you want to spend the rest of it? Perhaps you know the answer very clearly and are confidently pursuing God's direction for your life. But if you aren't sure, if you wonder about your purpose in the years ahead and how you might fulfill it, keep exploring the question, "Who am I, now that I've grown up?" It's a question you'll be glad you asked.

To analyze how your life has been shaped and the effect these experiences have had on your development, let's go back in time.

Identify Key Events

"One of the most life-shaping events that flashes into my mind is Bill's death," said Joan. A longtime friend of mine, Joan's husband had died in his early thirties. "When Bill was killed in a freak airplane accident, my secure world was demolished. Becoming a widow with two young sons to raise turned life upside down."

As a jumping-off point to knowing who you are today, and therefore being able to determine your direction for tomorrow, check your past. Search your memory to find those watershed events or people that have influenced your life. If some negative memories come to mind, don't block them out—write them down. Regardless of how you've handled them, they indeed shaped you. To stir up your memory bank, reflect on the following:

the circumstances of your birth and upbringing;
the kind of family life you had;
experiences in school: successful, painful, helpful;

people who influenced you, positively or negatively;
crises, losses, traumatic experiences; and
your journey as a Christian.

Now ask yourself:

What events or people stand out to me?
How did these events or people influence, affect, or change
    who I am and where I am today?

Write down your thoughts.

Probe Their Effects

The immediate effect of Joan's sudden plunge into wid-
owhood was having to face life alone. "In the first few days
after Bill's death, I had to make financial decisions I'd never
faced before," said Joan. "Although I was reeling from shock,
I had to focus my attention on helping my kids get through
the pain of losing their dad, forcing me to lay aside my own
loss—temporarily. Later on I had to look for a job, learn about
buying a house and car, and develop many other neglected
life-skills."

As the years went by and she remained single, Joan en-
dured a bout with breast cancer and reconstructive surgery
without a husband to lean on. At the same time, she helped
support her mother during her father's decline and death
from Alzheimer's disease. What effect have all these ham-
merblows had on Joan?

"After twenty-plus years as a widow, I'm now in mid-life,"
Joan said quietly. "As I look back I'm amazed at the skills

and strength God has given me. I doubt that many of them would have developed if my life had turned out as I had expected."

Having identified those life-shaping experiences and people in your own life, probe a little. Ask yourself:

What effect have events of my past had on me?
How have they helped to shape who I am today?

Record what you've discovered.

Evaluate for Direction

"When I think about what God has allowed me to go through," reflected Joan, "I want to be available to help others. By knowing what it's like to raise children without a father, I sense instant rapport with other single moms. Having been widowed, I know how hard it is to recover from a major loss, how long it takes. And, naturally, I understand the fears of women with breast cancer."

Rising slowly from the ashes of pain and grief, Joan's life is a powerful witness to God's faithfulness. As he brings hurting women across her path, her story infuses them with hope—they realize that they too can survive. The work of the Master Sculptor has not been in vain.

When you've pinpointed how the major events in your life have helped shape your direction, record your answers to these questions:

Have I developed a special sensitivity and concern for people who have been through similar experiences? Describe your thoughts and feelings.

Does God want to use my experiences for the sake of others? How might this occur?

How has God's shaping of me borne positive results in my life?

At mid-life, we need to take time to look back, pray for insight, and assess the path we've walked. Where has it led us? Who are we today? How do we use these experiences as building material for who we're going to be tomorrow? Will you head back to school for a counseling or nursing degree? Will you volunteer to be a child advocate or an ombudsman for an elderly person? How about changing your career field? As your mind soars with possibilities, keep your feet on the ground by gathering concrete information to assist you in your future plans.

My Jobs, Skills, Successes Tell Me . . .

What Have I Done in My Life?

Continue building your personal "This Is My Life" portfolio by doing the following exercise. Using another sheet of paper, divide your life into three chapters. In doing this exercise, I chose to divide my life in the following way:

Grade school through high school

High school to thirty-five years of age

Thirty-five to . . .

Choose whichever dividing points seem best to you. Inventory all the jobs you've held, including what you're doing currently. Be sure to catalog the jobs involved in running a home and caring for a family. And don't forget any volunteer work.

What Skills Do I Have?

Researchers who study the nature of skills divide them into three major categories: abilities to work with *people; information*—data and ideas; and *objects* or things such as tools and equipment.[3] As we look at these three categories, you might be surprised at how many skills you have and how many are transferable. In fact, they're like a bag of gold nuggets that you've mined from life—and now it's time to invest them for the best return. To unearth your own cluster of gold nuggets, let's do some panning and sifting and see what we find.

People Skills

Take a look at your job list and think about how you've interacted with people. Are you more comfortable working with individuals one at a time, or do you prefer being part of a group? Do you enjoy talking to your co-workers or neighbors? Do you like to encourage, give assistance, praise, and affirm? All these people skills are invaluable in any environment.

To get a grasp of your transferable skills in dealing with people, start cataloging those you've used or learned in each of the jobs you've listed. Here are some suggestions to stimulate your thinking. Title your list: *I am able to . . .*

Communicate my thoughts clearly.

Listen and hear what is being said.

Follow directions.

Settle conflicts.

Persuade, motivate, problem-solve.

Empathize, coordinate, instruct, encourage.

Information—Data and Idea Skills

Now consider those situations that utilize this next set of skills. Did you realize you use them all the time? Without recognizing it, we all use these skills every time we gather, analyze, or put information to use.

To get a handle on what it means to use data or idea skills, let's take grocery shopping as an example. When the fridge and the shelves are empty, you *think* about what you need and *write* down what to buy—unless your memory serves you better than most. At the market you *read* your list, *calculate* which brand is the better value, and then hand over your money—after wondering how it could possibly add up to that much. In running a home, organizing your life, or keeping track of your finances, you are analyzing information.

Search out your transferable strengths in this area by going back over your job list and writing down all the ways you interacted with data. To prod your memory, ask yourself, *Did I carry out any of the following responsibilities as a homemaker, volunteer, or paid employee? How else have I used this set of skills?* Start this list with the same title as before: *I am able to . . .*

Put together a budget.

Develop and implement ideas.

Keep track of details.

Gather information through research or observation.

Analyze data.

Implement action steps toward a goal.

Plan and organize.

Work with numbers.

Visualize and create.

Things and Object Skills

The third category of skills to assess are those that apply to physical objects that we use every day. For instance, I write on a computer, run a printer, and try to figure out how to make my fax modem work. Beyond that, my technical prowess is severely limited, even embarrassing.

After being advised by my husband not to drive on a slowly deflating tire, I stopped at a gas station hoping some helpful person would offer to pump it up for me. "The air is over there," said a singularly nonhelpful attendant, pointing across the lot.

Driving up as close as possible, I parked, leapt out, and tackled the tire. Unscrewing the air-nozzle (or whatever you call the thing that sticks out of a tire), I secretly applauded myself. At least I had accomplished step one.

Walking to the air machine, I tried to ignore the three people loitering by the nearby phone booth idly watching me. Grasping the rubber hose, I tugged and tugged until it was fully extended—two inches short of the tire. Nonchalantly,

I let the hose shoot back into the machine, climbed into my car, and reversed even closer.

This time the hose extended to the tire, but there was nothing on the end to attach to the tire's air-nozzle. Puzzled, I squatted on the ground holding it on the nozzle. Then, I saw the hose was dripping water. Jumping up, I strode back over to the machine and noticed, for the first time, that it had two hoses, one for air and one for water. Plus, you had to put a quarter in to activate either one.

Red with embarrassment, I quickly shoved a quarter into the machine, grabbed the proper hose, and screwed it onto the tire nozzle. Squirting air in the tire until it looked as fat as the others, I quickly finished the job and drove off.

My feelings of humiliation soon gave way to peals of laughter. Here I was, at mid-life, still struggling to figure out anything remotely technical.

Now that you know how limited my object-related skills are, take a look at your own. Start thinking about all the ways you use "hands-on" abilities. Take the following ideas as a jumping-off point, but be sure to note what else comes to mind. Again, title your list: *I am able to ...*

Create, fix, adjust, or repair objects.

Build, arrange, assemble—using tools, machines, or equipment.

Decorate, craft, sew, mold, shape, demonstrate, do precision work with my hands.[4]

Now that you've assessed your people, data, and object skills, look back over the information you've gathered so far. Then ask yourself the following, being sure to record your answers:

Which activities gave me the most fulfillment?
Exactly what contributed to my sense of fulfillment?
What activities did I dislike doing?
What does this tell me about myself?

I Feel Successful When . . . [5]

Let's continue discovering what gives you a sense of accomplishment and success. Take three pages in your journal:

On each page, record one of the age-spans you wrote down at the beginning of this chapter.

Under each age-span, write four accomplishments or successes that mattered to you during that time.

Your list might include doing well in school, adapting to difficult circumstances, excelling in a sport, or overcoming some handicap. Later, you may have held your marriage together through a tough time, served on the PTA, survived a severe loss, met a challenge, or succeeded in a demanding job.

Whatever stands out as something you feel good about, put it down. By the end of this exercise you should have a total of twelve events listed on your three pages.

Now go back over each of these. Using the list below as your guide, note the reasons why you feel this way.

1. I used my God-given skill and knowledge.
2. I was free to decide what I did or how I did it.
3. I influenced someone or got them to cooperate.
4. I helped someone else do something important to them.

5. I met a challenge or had an adventure.
6. I increased my self-respect.
7. I received money or other financial reward.
8. I received love and acceptance from my family or friends.
9. I learned something new.
10. I received recognition, support, or respect from others.

After noting why you felt a sense of success or accomplishment for each event you listed, look to see if one or two reasons predominate. Does a pattern emerge? What does it tell you about yourself?

As a final step in this self-discovery exercise, take the time to summarize what you've found. Write a definition:

A successful experience for me involves . . .

By finding out what gives you a sense of accomplishment and success, you've taken a major leap forward in knowing yourself. You've discovered what you value and what's important to you in order to have a sense of well-being. Using this information, you're on the way to answering that vital mid-life question, "Who am I, now that I've grown up?"

And What Do You Do . . . ?

"I've always thought of myself as a wife and mom," said Sally, "but the truth is, my children are gone, I'm separated from my husband, and I'm in the workforce. I guess it's time for me to rethink who I am. I need to know which roles are a part of my life and which aren't."

Whether you've spent the last few decades in the working world or predominately as a wife and mom, you've worn many hats. Think back over some of the roles you may have played: student, employee, mom, carpooler, room-mother, church member, teacher, friend, counselor, daughter, sister, wife. If we feel muddled in these middle years, part of it can be attributed to the bewildering shifts in our roles.

For some it's being called "Grandma" for the first time, for others it's struggling not to be the stereotypical mother-in-law. For many, it's reentering a working world that seems more foreign than Outer Mongolia, or facing the equally unfamiliar world of living as a single person after many years of marriage.

As our last exercise in discovering who you are, let's stop and look at the various roles or identities that are part of your life.

Write down ten roles you fill in your life.

Mark whether these are chosen, imposed, positive, or negative.

List them in order of their importance to you.

Record your thoughts on which roles best reflect how you see yourself.[6]

Some roles never change, such as being God's child, but others do. Letting go of an identity that no longer fits is a necessary step if you are going to move successfully through mid-life. Equally important is pinpointing which roles are of continuing value to you—those parts of your life that are worth retaining, whatever the effort.

Now that you've caught a glimpse of yourself by looking briefly at your personality, preferences, skills, and the roles you've played, you can answer more fully the question, "Who am I, now that I've grown up?" Aren't you delighted that you're definitely not who you were at the beginning of your first adult life-span? Instead, here you are, a more complex and capable woman than you've ever been, a person God invites to work with Him in whatever path lies before you. You've much to celebrate.

Having accumulated this fund of knowledge about yourself, you now face a decision—what will you do with it? Will you sit and navel-gaze, getting caught-up as our culture urges us to do in the fascinating pursuit of yourself? Or will you use all you know about yourself to make your life count? If you want to thrive in mid-life by investing in the years ahead, you need to answer the question, "Where do I go from here?"

10

Where Do I Go From Here?

"How can I possibly tell which way is north?" I responded incredulously to my husband as he gave me directions to an antiques mall. "In England people tell you to go right three miles till you come to some pub on the corner. Then they tell you to turn left, and after two more miles turn right again, and there you are. I don't know how to figure out where north is."

"It's perfectly simple," said Jim patiently. "You look at the sky and see where the sun is. Since it rises in the east and sets in the west, you check the time and if it's before noon . . ."

Baffled by this increasingly complex explanation, my mind raced ahead and spotted an obvious problem. "Ah!" I cried triumphantly. "What if it's night, or it's raining or snowing—

then what? Now tell me how I'm supposed to know where to go."

Don't you wish life had direction signs? Wouldn't it be easier if a billboard said Turn right five miles ahead and follow the nicely marked signs? Or if a map highlighted with fluorescent pink ink directed you down one road—until it intersected with exactly the right one heading a different way? By following the snaking pink trail across your map you'd have no trouble at all arriving exactly where you intended to go.

The only problem is this: God didn't create robots, and He doesn't hand out maps when we commit our lives to following Him. None of us goes through life conveniently preprogrammed to walk a certain path and perform without thinking. In His superior wisdom, God created living, intelligent human beings. He made us capable of analyzing various options, discerning what is best, desiring one way or another, and choosing what to do.

As members of the human race, we have freedom to make choices. As followers of Jesus Christ, our choices are set within the boundaries of what is pleasing to God.

"Seek first his kingdom and his righteousness, and all these things will be given to you as well," said Jesus. Echoing Jesus' challenge, Paul later exhorted believers, "Set your hearts on things above."[1]

In the Bible, God's manual for our journey through life, we find principles for *how* to live and *what* to live for. As our heavenly Father, God doesn't leave us in the dark regarding His broad goals and priorities for us. However, the detailed outworking of these is something that unfolds individually in each of our lives. As a unique and multifaceted person, your answer to the question, "Where do I go from here?" will reflect who you are.

As we continue our quest for direction, look back at what you've learned about yourself so far. Your fund of self-knowledge is building, but the picture isn't yet complete. By now you should have a good idea of what appeals to you and what you're good at doing. You probably also know what you don't want to spend time doing. At the top of my list is anything remotely technical.

In assessing where to go from here, let's add two more vital pieces of self-knowledge to your personal portfolio.

Discovering Your Passion: what motivates and excites you?

Determining Your Purpose: what are you living for?

Once your passion and purpose are clear, you're ready for the next step:

Developing Practical Life-Skills: setting goals, overcoming obstacles, and moving forward.

What's My Passion?

"I can't wait for Wednesday mornings to come around!" exclaimed Polly, her eyes shining with excitement. "I just love my 7:00 a.m. seminary class. It's so stimulating to discuss the nature of God and the different religious viewpoints."

You might not share Polly's particular passion, but there's probably something that motivates you to get out of bed extra early without grumbling. What makes your eyes sparkle? What makes your heart jump? That's *your* passion!

Passion, aliveness, and vitality spring from many sources. They're the fuel that feeds a sense of purpose and fulfillment. You can experience it when using your spiritual gift, making a difference in society or an individual's life, or channeling your whole self in some involvement that moves you deeply. Without it, life can easily become bland, dreary, and aimless.

To thrive in mid-life, you need to unlock your passion— the loves and activities God has uniquely shaped you to care about and make part of your life. As a first step toward this goal, give priority to knowing what gifts God has given you to use to build others up and bring you deep fulfillment.

Know Your Spiritual Gifting

Can you guess what spiritual gift feeds Polly's love of theology? If you answered "teaching," you're right. Do you know what yours is? Are you using it?

Spiritual gifts are special abilities God gives to every Christian. When you know your gifts and generously use them, other Christians are encouraged, non-Christians hear the Good News, and God's reality is expressed through your life. The result is joy for them *and* you.

How do we know what our particular gifts are? Does God expect us to search the sky for some divine sign, or does He boom down from heaven, "This is your spiritual gift" when we give our lives to Him? No, God doesn't play games with us. We can look in Scripture and find them clearly listed. In contrast to our usual way of thinking, however, we don't get to pick and choose what we want. Spiritual gifts are sovereignly given by the Holy Spirit according to His wishes, to be used for the common good.[2]

In trying to discern your spiritual gifts, the best place to start is with prayerful study of Romans 12:4–8; 1 Corinthians 12:4–7; and 1 Peter 4:10–11. When you've done this, record the following in your journal:

If and when you've exercised any of these gifts.

How you felt at the time and subsequently.

How people responded to the use of your gifts. Were you asked to contribute again?

How you spontaneously served God in some of these ways.

Are there other avenues of ministry that attract you? Make a note of them.

To summarize what you've been learning, write out your thoughts, beginning: *Energized by the Holy Spirit, I believe my spiritual gift (or gifts) is . . .*

If you're not sure where your spiritual strengths lie, ask some friends who know you well to tell you what they think. You can also look into resources that will help you gain more detailed and personal information about where you fit in the Body of Christ.[3] If you call your church office, you might find they have spiritual gift inventories available—and many places where your passion to serve can be used.

What Stirs Your Heart?

Do you blaze at racism, shudder at violence against women, ache for the loneliness of latchkey kids? Does the teen pregnancy rate or the polluted environment make you want to do *something*? Are you brokenhearted by the large number of abortions that occur each year or moved to tears by the plight of those without food or shelter? If so, you could be someone whose passion is fed by active participation in causes you feel strongly about.

On the other hand, maybe those aren't areas that move you deeply. You feel passion in more private pursuits, although not necessarily solitary ones.

Knowing what stirs your heart and pursuing it fully adds direction and vitality to life. Mother Teresa's passion to care for the poor and needy gave her strength to continue serving despite her age and health problems. Chuck Colson, ignited by concern for the spiritual and physical needs of those in prison, travels the globe on their behalf. Dr. James Dobson, fueled by a longing to equip today's families with Christian principles for living, uses every available means to assist Christians around the world. Passion motivates, infuses with energy and courage to step beyond the comfortable and familiar, and rewards with a sense of joy, meaning, and purpose.

What stirs you? Where would you like to invest your time in the years ahead? Where is God directing you?

In the muddled middle years, your passion might be directed toward others. Or it might be directed toward your own development. In either case, use the following as a jumping-off point for your thinking. Explore what you feel strongly about by recording it in your journal titled: *I'm stirred to action by* . . .

Directed toward others:

working for political reform;
loving, nurturing, or teaching children;
shepherding young believers, teens, singles;
teaching young moms homemaking and relational skills;
    or
helping women in crisis pregnancies.

Directed toward your own development:

achieving academic goals, learning new information;
starting a business by utilizing my skills;
pursuing my artistic bent to generate an income; or
moving up at work, being rewarded for my contribution.

Continue probing for your passion by asking yourself some key questions:

1. What do I do best?
2. Where do my interests lie?
3. What needs burden me?
4. In what area would I like to make a difference?
5. What career, job, or activity fits my skills and interests?
6. What excites and energizes me?
7. What do I sense God wants me to do?

If answers to these questions elude you, let them simmer gently on the back burner of your mind. Pray for insight and direction, and wait patiently. Whatever is at hand—do it. Let God, in His time, bring to the surface a focus for your life.

Perhaps you do know your passion, but the path toward living it out seems impossible. Take heart. God didn't shape you the way you are to let your dreams die. He knows His plans for you. They are for your good and His purposes.

Stay focused on praying, listening, and watching for His creative solutions. Nothing can stop God from doing what seems impossible, provided He generated your dream and passion.

Before you rush off in hot pursuit of what stirs you, however, you need to expand your vision of why you are here.

What's My Purpose in Life?[4]

"Who would like to share their purpose in life?" I asked the women attending my seminar on growing in mid-life. After a brief silence, Donna spoke up. "My purpose in life is to be a good wife," she said.

"If I'm honest, my purpose in life is to be a top executive in my company," admitted Betty with a shrug of her shoulders.

"Well, I have to admit I've never thought about a purpose in life," commented Alice. "I just take each day as it comes."

Do we need to have a purpose in life? Does having one make any difference? Will knowing your purpose help you make the best use of the years ahead? Yes, to all of the above. You need to know your purpose. It does make a difference. Knowing how you want to use your life provides a personal road map for your journey.

Living without a sense of purpose is like wandering around the supermarket purchasing items on impulse—on momentary appeal. Once you get home, though, you realize that your purchases don't add up to the kind of meal you meant to fix.

You could also liken a lack of purpose to those fun (and probably rare) times when you go shopping for a whole new wardrobe. You pick a blouse in one color, a skirt in another, a jacket or pants in other hues, but instead of several coordinating outfits, you're muttering, "I've got nothing to wear." You have parts that are individually pleasing, but you haven't achieved your desired objective.

Abraham Maslow devoted his life to the study of human psychology. In his research on what motivates and satisfies people, he discovered that the quality and quantity of our lives is directly affected by a sense of purpose *felt at mid-life.*[5]

In seeking direction during this time of shifting roles, inner stirrings, and questions about the future, stop and think about your purpose. Perhaps your immediate response echoes Donna's: "My purpose is to be a good wife." Maybe you identify more with Betty, whose primary focus was advancing in her career.

Without realizing it, we can easily cling to inadequate and temporary substitutes as a reason to live. Donna is not guaranteed a husband all her days. If she finds herself alone, what would be her purpose for living? Betty may find herself a casualty of downsizing or unable for a number of reasons to achieve her dream. *Then* what does she live for?

To tie your sense of purpose to family, career, possessions, or prestige is to link your reason for living to something that can easily slip away. Although many of these common life-anchor points are deeply satisfying, they are all inadequate and temporary substitutes for a sense of purpose that covers the unknowns of life. Unlike goals that are measurable, accomplishable, and when achieved replaced by other goals, a sense of purpose provides a fixed point from which to make decisions.

Jesus knew why he was on the earth and what he was to accomplish. All of his choices contributed to his life purpose. He said that his food (satisfaction) was to do the will of God. For that reason he didn't seek to please himself while on earth, but rather the One who sent him. As a result of his clear focus, just before he went to Gethsemane and Golgotha, Jesus could declare, "I have completed the work you gave me to do."[6]

What we accomplish on earth bears no comparison with Christ's mission, but our purpose does have some similarities if we are his followers.

Purpose has an eternal perspective.

Purpose gives deep satisfaction.

Purpose touches other people's lives for good.

Purpose transcends life's ups and downs.

Knowing your ultimate mission in life enables you to go on, even if you lose precious relationships, financial security, health, or any other seemingly indispensable part of life. God wants us to have an impelling sense of why we are here on earth—and to live purpose-driven lives. When we know our purpose, we can begin to set goals and answer the question, "Where do I go from here?"

Bob Shank, author of *Total Life Management*, suggests that a life purpose should answer two questions: "Why do I exist?" and "How do I glorify God?"

Our purpose, or mission, should be the same as that of Jesus Christ—to glorify God. It's easy for Christians to agree with that. But how do we make it personal? How do we translate that general objective into a clear focus for our own future?

To create your own life-purpose statement, work through the following in your journal:

Sifting through all the self-knowledge you've accumulated so far, what patterns of interest do you see?

Which of these repeated activities reflect your heart priorities?

Are you drawn to something that up until now you haven't been able to fit into your life?

As I worked through this exercise, my own answers revealed consistent involvement in teaching life-applicable truth from Scripture and counseling, writing, and training women in various aspects of Christian leadership. I also felt a strong desire to continue in these areas. What did you find?

To complete this exercise, you need to take two last steps:

Drawing on what you've just written down, begin to simplify your reflections. Then work through these thoughts until you can express your life's purpose in one sentence.

Begin your statement with: "My life purpose is to . . ." and end it, "for the glory of God."[7]

Recognizing the key heart-involvements that characterize my life, my statement reads: "My life purpose is to stir others to hunger and thirst after God, for His glory."

Facing the years ahead with a clear sense of my life purpose, I know how I want to use my time. I don't know the details of where, when, or how, but I do know *what* God has given me to do for Him.

Your statement will reflect your uniqueness. Perhaps it is to enrich the lives of a particular group of people, to build relationships for the purpose of sharing the gospel, to encourage wise stewardship of our planet. As you formulate your life purpose statement, remember, you're not establishing a goal which, once attained, is replaced by another. You are expressing, in a broad sense, how you genuinely want to use your life.

Not knowing the future, however, you might find that your purpose undergoes some fine-tuning or even redefinition as you or your circumstances change. If this should happen, just make the necessary adjustments and go on.

Lasting as long as you're capable of making choices for yourself, your personal purpose statement becomes a steady plumb line against which to measure the value of a beckoning path. It also becomes your compass, a reliable guide for your onward journey.

So far, all the exercises you've worked on have built toward establishing your prime purpose in life. Now let's turn our attention to setting goals and acquiring some useful problem-solving tools.

Where Do I Go From Here?

How old will you be five years from now? Take a moment and think about who and where you want to be by that age. In the next five years you can do nothing, *or* you can choose to dream, set goals, risk, and expand your horizons. Either way, you will be five years older. That birthday might find you dissatisfied, restless, and wondering, *Is this all there is to life?* Or you could find yourself invigorated and purpose-directed, looking back at a satisfying stretch of life.

Goal-setting is answering the question, "What will it take to go from where I am to where I want to be?" If we're serious about submitting our lives to God, we'll always add, "If it is the Lord's will" to all our goals. Only He knows what each day will bring.[8]

With that in mind, let yourself begin to dream about the following:

Long-range goals—what would you like to accomplish in the next five to twenty years?

Mid-range goals—in two to five years from now, what targets will you aim for to help you achieve your long-range goals?

Short-range goals—in the next two years, what specific, measurable targets will help you meet your mid-range goals?

Give yourself time to pray and mull over your long-range goals. They should reflect your passion and purpose. Once you've identified them, they provide direction and focus for your short- and mid-range goals. Knowing your destination will help you move forward, overcome inevitable obstacles, provide structure, and keep you on track. And as you check off each accomplishment along the way, you'll be delighted by all God has enabled you to do.

In a previous chapter I mentioned my friend Carol. She is a forty-something college student with a long-range goal of becoming a licensed counselor. She's highly motivated as a Christian to achieve her goal of helping families with their problems. In addition, Carol hopes her future career will provide finances for her children's education and be a source of personal satisfaction and fulfillment. But Carol's not unrealistic about the costs involved. She grapples with time pressures, money pressures, hard work, and fatigue. She has little energy left for friends or herself.

As you peer down the road into the future, start adding some goals to your personal portfolio. Whatever you ultimately settle on, your goals need to line up with your commitment to God and the responsibilities He has given you.

To begin this important project, put a new title in your journal: *Goal Planning*. If that's too boring, call it whatever inspiring or exotic title you can think of. The important thing is you're starting to map where you want to go in your second adult life-span—an exciting idea. List the following, allowing room for filling in your responses:

What is my long-range goal (or goals)?
This needs to be specific, measurable, achievable, rewarding, and tangible. (To look like you're twenty, for example, is specific—but it's not achievable!)

What are the benefits of achieving this goal?

175

Will it help me more fully use my abilities? Will it meet some definite needs? Will others be helped in some way?

What personal or external obstacles might I face?

What are some possible solutions?

What specific action steps do I need to take?

How will I monitor my progress?

What target dates will I set for each step? What supportive person could I be accountable to?

Is it worth my time, money, and effort to do this?[9]

These guidelines for goal-setting can be used in every area of your life. Whether you're planning your future direction or trying to rid yourself of a firmly entrenched bad habit, use this tool to help you get to where you want to go.

Once Carol had sifted through all the possibilities before her and decided what direction to take, she listed six specific action steps toward her long-term goal. These steps covered three years and began with finding out which degree program she should enroll in. She then listed five more steps: getting financial aid, finishing thirty credits, transferring from junior college to the local university, graduating, and getting a job in her chosen field.

Juggling school, family, and other necessary commitments, Carol feels no small pressure as she works to stay on target. But she is also thriving as she moves toward achieving her personal dreams for tomorrow.

If you find yourself hesitating to frame some goals for yourself, think through the following:

What Am I Waiting For?[10]

The right person to come along?

The children to grow up?

Somebody to take care of me?

To finish my education?

Someone to notice my plight?

Someone to offer me a job?

My financial problems to end?

Something bad to happen?

Someone else to change?

Someone else to make the decision?

Someone to discover me?

What else?

What is the probability that what I'm waiting for will really happen?

What is happening while I am waiting?

Where do I think I will end up if I just continue waiting?

What can I do now to stop waiting and start moving forward to find out what God wants in my life?

Once you've determined to begin working toward your goals, expect to encounter some tough places along the way. You might well be tempted to quit, to settle for whatever seems easier, but the path to anything worthwhile is usually uphill—at least part of the time.

When you're aware of problems or obstacles blocking your way, take time to investigate where they're coming from and what solutions are possible. The sooner you do this, the faster you'll be able to shed their nagging shadow. For some guidelines to assist you, work through the following.

Basic Steps to Problem-Solving[11]

1. Remember that you don't need to face your problems alone—ask God to help you throughout this process.
2. Acknowledge that there is a problem, a reason for your discomfort.
3. Define the problem. What needs are going unmet?
4. Determine whose problem it is.
5. List possible solutions.
6. Analyze the possible solutions. What are their advantages and disadvantages?
7. Choose the best solution to *your* problem.
8. Put your choice into action.
9. Set a date and choose a process to evaluate whether or not your solution has worked.

By now you've amassed an invaluable collection of very personal glimpses of who you are. You also have important decisions to make.

At mid-life, you stand at a crossroads weighing which path to take. At this momentous time in your life, don't lose your sense of anticipation and adventure by fearing you might make a wrong choice. If you discover something else lights up your eyes and makes you hop eagerly out of bed early in the morning, pursue your passion. After all, hasn't it always been a woman's prerogative to change her mind?

So far we've focused on striding enthusiastically into our second adulthood. But we also need to take a realistic look at our own aging. How do we prepare for that season of life hovering like a mirage in the far distance? To find out how to get ready for being *really* old, let's identify some basic steps we need to take now.

11

How Do I Get Ready
for Being *Really* Old?

"My dear, these years of caring for your children will pass so quickly. They'll be grown and gone before you know it." The understanding voice of Edye, a middle-age mother of four, floated softly over my shoulder as I wrestled with my squirming two-year-old son in the church nursery.

Elliot didn't want to have his diaper changed, and I didn't feel like doing it, either. Quite frankly, I was tired of diapers—and scrubbing oatmeal off the walls, breaking up toy-snatching squabbles, and trying to corral a toddler and preschooler whenever we went out the door. *I don't see the years passing quickly at all*, I thought wearily. *In fact, I can't imagine my life ever being any different.* How wrong I was.

If the past twenty years have sped by like a fast-paced action movie, dare we believe that the next twenty or forty won't do the same? Look back at what formed the core of your life approximately twenty years ago—was it small children, college classes, early career steps? Think about the changes you've experienced in the past two decades. Now face reality—in the future you'll be looking back twenty years, and these are the years you'll reminisce about.

Believing that time will stand still and we'll never get *really* old is a comforting illusion. At mid-life, many of us feel much too young to be the age we are, and imagining ourselves as seventy-somethings or eighty or ninety is way beyond our grasp. But it will happen, unless we die early.

Once we've stopped cowering in a corner hiding from this fact, what should we anticipate and get ready for? Well, assuming that the years continue to click off relentlessly, if you're working, one day you will retire. If you have a husband, at some point he will be at home—possibly all day. If you have children, they might marry and make you not only a mother-in-law, but also a grandma. You might even find yourself the full-time caretaker of your grandchildren.

As wise and mature women who've been willing to accept that we're in mid-life, let's also face the far future without denial. In addition to all the positive and exciting possibilities dotting the landscape of the next few decades, being realistic means we must acknowledge the possibility of negative changes in our health, marital, or financial status. Because of these and other potential adjustments that could lie ahead, what do we need to do *now* for the greatest peace of mind regarding tomorrow? How can we avoid anxiety about our later years, being unprepared either for crisis or for chronic difficulties?

To blossom and flourish in the future, rather than wither and perish before our time, we need to work now. None of us can assume our old age will be problem-free or wait for its arrival before deciding on crucial issues. Our economic, emotional, and physical welfare as "little old ladies" depends on making thoughtful decisions in these middle years.

Plan for Tomorrow

Once upon a time there was no such thing as retirement. People were considered old at forty. They worked hard, had meager savings, and pensions were little known. Staying in the workforce was essential for survival.[1]

Today's upbeat view of retirement and aging visualizes the later years as a seedpod, plump with exciting possibilities. On bursting open, seeds shower in every direction, scattering across our lives. Taking root, they colorfully sprinkle our later years with joy and renewed energy.

It goes without saying that we all hope this will be our experience. In my fantasies about old age, I imagine myself crackling with energy and enthusiasm. Strapping on my in-line skates, I zip past middle-aged ladies plodding along on their daily walk. They watch, astounded, as I race up and down the street, my wrinkled face creased into a wide smile. And when I do a cartwheel . . .

But back to reality. To get ready for being *really* old, project yourself forward in time.

Step Into the Future ...

Unleash your imagination and picture yourself living through what you think will be a typical day as a seventy-year-old. You might not want to do this exercise, but do it anyway! What you'll soon uncover are the expectations you have for yourself as an older woman.

Think about your health—are you battling problems now that might be worse then? What activities do you expect to be involved with? What about the number of friends you'll have? Where do you see yourself living—in your current home, a smaller place, in the sunbelt? What will your expenses be? How much will you have to live on? Will family or close friends be nearby?

The picture you've formed by mulling over these questions reveals some of your expectations for tomorrow. Your view may be optimistic or pessimistic, depending on various influences. Your feelings about the future are colored by how you see life today, whether you'll be ready financially for the retirement years, your health status and that of family members, and how you plan to use your time. The experiences of your parents or other relatives in their later years also influence your thinking about growing old.

Of course, there's no way to know what you will experience, but you can take definite steps to prepare yourself for what's coming.

Figure Out Your Finances

Where does all your money go? Do you know? Can you come up with a ballpark figure of the net worth of your household? Could you find financial, tax, and investment documents if you needed to? Getting ready for being *really* old involves grappling with some rather mundane facts and figures, but we're foolish if we neglect to educate ourselves.

1. Determine your net worth.[2]

Planning for the future requires knowing what you own and what you owe. To do this, calculate your net worth and your total debt.

What do I (we) own? Include cash, bank balances, savings, bonds, life insurance cash value, mutual funds, other investments, retirement plans, pension funds, market value of your home, other real estate, equity in a business, cars, household goods, debts owed to you.

What do I (we) owe? List mortgage payments, current bills, credit card balances, taxes due, debts you owe others.

The difference between what you own and what you owe is your net worth.

2. Record your monthly income and expenses.

In addition to knowing your net worth, sound financial planning involves tracking exactly what monies come in each month and what goes out. Doing this can help you find more places to save money and increase the amount you are putting away for retirement. If wisely invested, these dollars will accumulate and bring much appreciated returns in your later years.

Sources of income: Wages or salary, interest, dividends, proceeds from sales, rents on property, profits, repayment of loans.

Fixed expenses: Rent or mortgage, fees, taxes, utilities, payments on loans or credit cards, insurance, transportation, membership dues, charitable giving, tuition, subscriptions, savings and investments.

Flexible expenses: Food, meals away from home, clothing, laundry and dry cleaning, furniture or household purchases, maintenance and repair, home improvements, supplies, gifts, vacations, health expenses, personal care, entertainment, recreation, etc.

Detailing what you take in and what you spend on a monthly basis tells you your current financial situation. Now think ahead. What will you need for living expenses when you and/or your spouse are no longer earning a regular paycheck?

3. Estimate your future financial needs.

Will you still be paying your mortgage when you're retired? What will your income be apart from Social Security? How often will you need a new car? How many trips do you hope to take each year? What about your clothes budget? Will you need supplemental insurance policies?

Even if your mind swims when faced with columns of figures, force yourself to think logically about your present and future financial status. If you haven't already, read about financial planning for your future years, attend retirement seminars, and consult a professional for help.[3]

In her article "How to Live Worry-Free When You Retire," Penelope Wang points out that one of every two women over sixty-five is divorced or widowed. Furthermore, "forty percent of women receiving Social Security rely on it for at least 90 percent of their income." The result? Three-quarters of the elderly poor are women.[4]

Anxiety and panic are not helpful responses to these dismaying statistics. Praying, thinking, and taking action in the middle years are what's needed.

If you're married and have paid little attention to financial matters, talk to your husband about the importance of knowing where you stand financially. Maybe knowing your financial picture will be just the incentive you need to avoid that super-special sale at the mall.

Be Prepared for Crisis[5]

If your husband were given a grave diagnosis or dies unexpectedly, what would you do? Have you discussed what immediate action to take if a crisis hits—whom to contact, what forms to file, whom to turn to for financial, legal, and personal advice? What if you were to divorce?

For peace of mind, prepare yourself before you encounter a crisis. Here are some areas that need attention now:

Access to cash for immediate expenses.

Access to bank accounts and your safe-deposit box.

Joint ownership of your house, stock certificates, his business.

Assets in your name only.

Medical insurance, disability, long-term care coverage. Do your policies reflect today's costs? What is the deductible for catastrophic care?

Information about all savings, investments, pension, and other retirement monies.

Developing a crisis plan incorporating the above.

Thinking about life's painful possibilities is necessary. Planning ahead won't remove your grief, but it will insure that you're not left bewildered and susceptible to poor advice. You owe it to yourself and your family to be ready if tragedy strikes.

Put Your Wishes in Writing

Do you want your favorite sister to get the old family piano? Your second daughter to have a special piece of jewelry, or your youngest son to inherit the grandfather clock that belonged to your father? When wishes and intentions aren't written down, family quarrels and hard feelings frequently occur. Even more serious, when your desires regarding end-of-life issues are not recorded, confusion and guilt feelings often result.

1. Decide where your estate goes.

Experts strongly advise everyone to have an up-to-date will to avoid delays and difficulties for the family of the deceased. In spite of this, two thirds of all Americans still die without having completed one.[6]

No matter how poor you think you are, you have assets that form your estate. Whether single or married, talk to an attorney and draw up a will. By doing this, you can discuss how to avoid excess taxes, and you can specify how your assets should be distributed.

2. Specify end-of-life decisions.

Living wills. Call your local hospital for information about a living will. This legal document allows you to specify your wishes regarding extraordinary measures to be taken in the event of a terminal condition.

Power of attorney. This permits someone you choose to act as your agent if you become incapacitated. By combining a living will with a power of attorney, a person you trust is designated to act on your behalf when medically necessary.[7]

Your funeral wishes. When you're in a particularly upbeat mood, tackle one more end-of-life issue—think about your funeral. I've told my husband who I want to conduct my funeral—a favorite preacher who lives nearby. Unfortunately, because of his age, he might be gone long before I need him.

On several occasions in the middle of singing in church or listening to a tape of old hymns, I've turned to my husband and said, "Don't forget. I want this hymn sung at my funeral." But I know that unless I write it down and put it with those terribly somber documents we all need to have in one place, no one will sing my favorites.

Do you have any special wishes or strong feelings you want known and carried out? Are there certain people you want officiating or involved in some way? Put it down on paper.

Get Ready for New and Changed Relationships

Help, I'm a Mother-in-law!

From the time your son or daughter starts dating, you're in training to become a mother-in-law. And looking down the road to when you're a little old lady, remember that your relationship with your son- or daughter-in-law *then* is being established *now*.

How can you avoid the dreaded stereotype of the unwanted, interfering, and critical mother-in-law? Learn from those who've walked that path.

Keep your views to yourself. "When my daughter told me she and her husband were buying a dog, I kept my opinion to myself," said Helen. "I knew they didn't have time to care for it, and that once it outgrew the puppy stage they'd have a problem on their hands. But it wasn't my place to tell them what to do. I figured this experience would help them to avoid such impulsive decisions in the future. As it turned out, I was right. After only one month, their puppy had a new home."

Refrain from criticizing their choices. "Sherrie and her husband don't want to have any children," sighed Pauline. "Their only interest seems to be accumulating money and a fancy car and house. It's hard not to be critical of their choices and how they use their money, but saying something would only alienate them."

Remain neutral. Joyce loves her son, Tim, but doesn't feel close to Janet, her daughter-in-law. "Even though I might feel Tim is right, when he and Janet have disagreements I refuse to take sides," she said. "If Tim complains about her, I listen, but don't make any negative comments. They need to work out their problems without me becoming one of them. After all, they *are* adults."

Fit in with their schedules. "My in-laws park their trailer in our yard for six weeks every year," griped Karol. "Tom and I are never going to impose ourselves like that on our kids.

"We've told our children that we'd love to visit them but they need to consider their schedules and invite us to come. We're not inviting ourselves or expecting them to put us up whenever we want to be with them."

Establish financial boundaries. Joan and her husband, Peter, built a successful business. Money is not a problem for them, and they are happy to assist their children in purchasing a first home. They've also discussed with their children plans to set aside money in a trust fund for the grandchildren's education.

Being able to help your children finance major investments is something many parents wish to do, but having money can also be extremely divisive.

"Our daughter and her husband constantly drop hints about their financial struggles," commented Mary. "We're generous toward all three of our children and their spouses, but we refuse to bail them out of their financial problems. They have to take responsibility for their own choices and take care of their own families. Recently I decided to set boundaries on myself when I go shopping with my daughter. It's so easy to keep spending on her or the grandchildren. Without meaning to, I think I contributed to our children expecting constant handouts."

Honey, I'm Home . . . for Breakfast, Lunch, and Dinner

"Bob is driving me crazy," groaned Dottie to her friend Eleanor. "Ever since he retired he's been following me around like a puppy dog. He's even rearranged all my kitchen cabinets because he thinks it will help me work more efficiently."

"It's just the opposite for me," responded Eleanor. "I just love having Harold around, even though it is a major adjustment. He worked such long hours and traveled so much all the years of our marriage, I couldn't wait for him to retire so we could spend more time together."

When husbands retire, a wife's life is changed forever—for better or worse. But, with forethought and graciousness, it needn't be a grating experience.

Getting ready for being *really* old means talking to your spouse about the inevitable adjustments you will both face.

If you're still working outside the home, will you retire also? If not, what extra household chores will your husband take on? When you're both at home each day, what activities will you do together and which will you pursue separately?

The initial months, and possibly years, of retirement usher in enormous changes. By stepping out of his familiar routine, your husband will face difficult adjustments—often in the form of painful losses. Retirement brings the end of camaraderie with co-workers, acknowledgment of his capabilities, structure to his day, and a regular income.

You too will face major changes in your routine—not least, what to fix for breakfast, lunch, and dinner. You could, of course, assign him lunch duty . . . and maybe dusting, bedmaking, or the ironing.

Even though a different or more leisurely pace of life has enormous appeal, retirement remains a major life transition. It's impossible to go through such enormous changes without some degree of difficulty. Reminding yourself of this on a daily (or hourly) basis will help you weather those rocky adjustments that give birth to new routines.

Congratulations! You're a Grandmother

"Would you like to see a few photos of my grandchildren?" "My seven-year-old grandson, Jeremy, is so smart. He's way ahead of the others in his class." "Oh, look at Melissa. She dances so beautifully, I know she'll become a professional ballerina."

Bragging, pride, or normal grandmotherly delight? Whichever it is, if you have children, you'll quite likely find yourself a grandmother when you're really old. You might even be one already.

Whether you become a grandma in early mid-life or in your senior-citizen-discount years, it's unlikely you'll fit the stereotypical pink-faced, snowy-haired, cookie-baking, chubby old lady. Well, not until you've lived a few more decades at least.

Today's grandmothers are smart cookies themselves. Busy, attractive, and healthier than ever before, most utter cries of delight over those sweet little bundles of joy produced by their offspring. With love at first sight, a new relationship is born—not only with your grandchild, but also with your adult child.

Mom, You're a Terrific Grandma

In their book *Grandparenting With Love and Logic*, authors Foster Cline, MD, and Jim Fay address contemporary grandparenting issues.[8] They divide grandparents into three categories:

Helicopters: they hover around making protective noises, swoop down and rescue when help is needed, and willingly set aside their own plans to babysit at a moment's notice.

Drill Sergeants: they bark orders, give put-downs, tease unkindly, make threats, tell their kids how to parent.

Consultants: they listen, give choices, sympathize, but don't rescue or interfere.

No doubt we'd all like to be the perfect grandmother—the consultant who sensitively relates to our grandchildren as well as to their parents. Clearly, being a model grandma requires as much or more tact than being a mother-in-law. By adding children to the family mix of various adults trying to get along, the potential for intergenerational squabbles increases by leaps and bounds.

For family harmony, practice "good mother-in-law" principles. In addition, respect your child's role as parent, and determine not to give unasked-for advice, especially in front of little eyes and ears.

Early on, make a point of discussing your role as a grandparent with them. Invite them to share their desires and expectations of you. In turn, state your thoughts and desires, especially regarding babysitting, visiting their home, and being a spiritual influence on their child.

Full-time grandparenting. As a result of death, divorce, abandonment, drug abuse, and other difficulties, caring for a grandchild on a full-time basis is no longer unusual. Census Bureau figures show that more than three million children in the United States now live with their grandparents.[9]

Only you, together with your spouse, can make such an enormous personal decision if faced with the heartbreak of grandchildren needing a home. Before responding out of understandable emotion, ask yourself if this is the best decision for them and for you. What alternatives are possible? Have you consulted child-care professionals for advice? Have you talked to a lawyer? Are you able to do this—physically, emotionally, and financially?

In weighing what to do, talk with wise friends or others who have faced this situation. There are also organizations especially set up to help grandparents in your situation. Seek out the sound advice and support they have to offer.[10]

I Wish You Lived Closer, Grandma

If you live in the same town as your grandchild, you're the envy of many. But even living a thousand miles away or in another country can't stop you from being the joy of your grandchild's heart. Let's find out how.

Stay in touch. Make regular phone calls at a specific time, write letters just to them, send little treasures you find that remind you of them. Chat or sing to them on tape, record tales of when you were their age, read Bible stories as well as other stories. Tell them why God is real to you and how you pray for them.

Plan celebrations. If you can't be with your grandchild for Christmas or some other special event, send a videotape of greetings and activities. Decide to have family reunions and set the dates a year or two ahead. In the interim, tell your grandchildren stories about their various relatives. Invent your own reasons to celebrate and festively share these through mailing special foods, crafts, or small gifts.

Tuck a camera in your purse and snap pictures during walks or on trips. Get a friend to take pictures of you shopping or in your garden. Place these in an album, with simple captions underneath telling what you're doing, and you've created a keepsake for your grandchild.

Being a grandma is one of the joys of growing older. And what could be sweeter than having an admirer who believes you can answer all of life's mysteries?

Now that we've covered the basics of getting ready for being *really* old, let's focus on today. Thriving in these muddled middle years is our goal. But what produces and feeds a zest, a spirit of vitality, and a sense of fulfillment during mid-life and even beyond? Let's move on and uncover what will make the difference between merely surviving and truly thriving.

12

I'm Not Just Surviving,
I'm Thriving

"Mom, Carolyn can only spend two weeks backpacking with me in Europe," said my daughter, Malaika, with a sigh of disappointment. "I was hoping we could travel together for a month after I graduate. Now it looks like I'll have to sight-see on my own for the second two weeks."

Like most devoted mothers with overactive imaginations, alarming scenes immediately flooded my mind. Picturing my daughter crying out, "Mom, save me!" while being carried off by some fiend, I quickly moved into action. Without a moment's reflection, I blurted out, "Well, I'd be happy to go with you if you'd like me to."

Jim looked up from his newspaper in shock and amazement. "*You* are offering to *backpack*? *You*, the one who needs two suitcases and your hairdryer and *me* to help you manage when we take a trip? *You* are going to carry everything you need for two weeks on your back?"

Laughing at Jim's utter disbelief, I said, "Well, other women my age do it, so why can't I?"

"It sounds great to me, Mom," chimed in Malaika. "You're too old to stay in youth hostels, so I'll have to share your hotel room." Her delighted smile told me she'd instantly recognized the financial benefits of having her mother along for two weeks.

Planning and dreaming about my mid-life backpacking venture, stimulating and exciting in itself, was just the beginning.

Six months later, lugging my backpack through Paris's Charles de Gaulle Airport, I headed for an automatic teller machine to get some French currency. On reaching the machine, my mind froze—there were no letters on the keypads, only numbers. I remembered my code word but I couldn't think how to translate it into numbers. Wildly stabbing at the keys I hoped would spell my code word, I watched in panic as the screen said *Incorrect, try again.*

Half an hour later, clutching my useless automatic teller card and cash from a traveler's check, I bought a train ticket into Paris. Malaika and Carolyn were to meet me at the ticket booth in the train station. On arriving at the station, I experienced my second wave of panic—there were a dozen ticket booths on various levels and in all directions. How would we ever find each other, and if we didn't, what was the name of our hotel? I had no idea. The girls had booked it and planned to meet me at the station and take me there.

Exhausted from the overnight flight and upset with myself for assuming we'd have no problems meeting up, I went from booth to booth for nearly two hours, willing myself not to cry. Finally, too tired to keep looking, I sank down onto the cold, marble floor of the dirty station, praying fervently for God's help. A short while later Malaika found me.

"Mom, where've you been?" Malaika exclaimed in relief as she spotted me sitting like a bag lady, arms tightly wrapped around my backpack. "We've been looking everywhere for you. I called Dad back in the States and woke him up. I told him you were lost, and we didn't know what to do. Thank goodness we've found you."

With hugs and tears of relief all around, we agreed we'd made a huge mistake in not communicating more clearly.

The next day, staggering down a Paris street under a load that made me look like the Hunchback of Notre Dame, I began to wonder what had possessed me to come on a trip where I had to carry everything on my back. My neck bulged, my shoulder blades met in the middle, and I struggled to reach around my backpack to hoist it up.

"Are you okay, Mom?" Malaika called to me as I trudged single file behind her through throngs of tourists. "Sure, I'll make it," I muttered through clenched teeth.

And I did. In fact, once I ignored the feeling that I was about to keel over and lie wedged in a Paris gutter for the rest of my life, I swelled with justifiable pride. *Here I am*, I thought, *a middle-age woman, backpacking for the first time in my life. And I'm not just surviving, I'm doing great. I'm really able to do this. Whoever would have thought it possible?*

On reflection, would I step out of the familiar and comfortable again and do something so out of character for me? Yes. Would I plan more carefully next time? Definitely.

Accomplishing something I never envisioned myself doing was exhilarating. True, it wasn't smooth sailing all the way. And it doesn't matter that someone else might find my experience of little consequence. What matters is that I pushed myself beyond my own self-imposed limits and beliefs about my capabilities. In doing this, I discovered not only that I could do more than I thought, but now my appetite for challenging myself was whetted. So who knows what I might attempt next? Maybe that elephant ride through the jungles of Thailand needs a second thought.

Surviving or Thriving?

Taking risks and being willing to stretch yourself beyond what's familiar is one way to thrive in the adventure of life. But how do we thrive on the routine days? After all, let's be realistic. Most of us live fairly mundane lives and aren't going to be bungee-jumping or traveling in remote areas on a regular basis. Does that mean, then, that we have no choice but to settle for ho-hum lives, watching the years add up until it's all over? Of course not.

Living as fully as possible on a daily basis is not only a worthwhile goal, it's God's design. As our Creator, He knows what we need in order to thrive physically, mentally, emotionally, and spiritually. And it should come as no surprise to discover that much current research in the area of happiness and well-being for a long life supports what has always been there in Scripture.

What's needed for a sense of zest, revitalization, energy, and well-being? Here are eight essentials for a life that has both substance and sizzle. Put these building blocks in place and you'll not merely survive the middle years—you'll thrive.

1. Cultivate Your Relationship With God

Mid-life is not only a time of change, it's prime time to think about your relationship with God. Research shows that people who are actively religious are happier than those who aren't.[1] Other studies affirm that a sense of well-being comes from living out your values—knowing what really matters to you and putting it into practice. If you are a Christian, this means cultivating what you claim really matters to you—your relationship with God. If you are in the process of wondering whether God is real, or if Jesus Christ is who He claims to be, mid-life is the time for deliberate exploration.

Long-term interactions between people often lose fresh, dynamic input. And, without intending it to happen, even the best marriage can become a boring routine. The same can be true in your relationship with Jesus Christ.

Couple a hectic lifestyle with the worries of everyday living, and the time we need for spiritual nourishment often becomes almost nonexistent. Our sensitivity to God shrivels. We slowly settle for a stale, perfunctory relationship, disconnected from our real concerns.

If you want to thrive spiritually in the years ahead, take an honest look at where you are in your relationship with God today. If you are a Christian, you need to reestablish the lordship of Jesus Christ at the core of your life, to revitalize your awareness of why you are here and whose you are. You need to regain the deep sense of well-being that comes from a close walk with God. If, as a person curious about God, this idea of a close walk with a personal God intrigues you, don't smother your questions. Ask a Christian friend to tell you more.

To spark a sluggish spiritual life, here's a potpourri of ideas:

Read the Manual

Spend a minimum of fifteen minutes daily on an appointment with God. Read a few verses or a chapter from a modern translation of the Bible, reflect on what it says, and record your response in a notebook. God uses His Word to reveal himself, so what is He saying to you? Ask Him for insights.

Probe the passage for what it teaches about God. How does it address your life circumstances? Is there a comforting promise or a biblical principle to apply? What about attitudes that need to be changed? Write out your response as a prayer.

Read several of the praise Psalms, amplifying any praise-filled statements about God with your own words. Feed the flame of your passion for God by reading a spiritually meaty devotional each day *in addition* to God's Word. Ask friends which ones have drawn them closer to God.

You might like to meet regularly with another woman, perhaps over your lunch hour or for coffee, for the specific purpose of exchanging what you are each learning as you read through a book of the Bible.

To help you keep focused and challenged in your Bible-reading, try working through a study guide in your daily time with God. Ask friends who study the Bible for themselves or check with a church librarian for suggestions.

Perk Up Your Prayer Life

Buy or borrow a book on prayer—after all, it's hard to be motivated to pray if you don't know what good it does or why you should.

Practice praying aloud or write out your prayers. Both help you to concentrate. You can pray constantly by talking to God as a friend about each situation and concern. When you feel delighted by the scenery, the kindness of an acquaintance, the sweetness of a child, the successful accomplishment of a difficult task, express your thanks and praise to God.

To help you see how God answers prayer, write your prayer requests and put a date beside them. Pray expectantly based on a Scripture promise, remembering that God sometimes answers no or "not yet." You can also ask a friend to be your prayer partner.

Do you know that you can pray for insight into problems *you* face, for changes *you* need to make in yourself, as well as for the needs of others? God cares about *you*, too.

Seek Out Spiritual Companions

Dump the Lone Ranger syndrome—the Scriptures command believers to love, encourage, exhort, pray with, and bear one another's burdens. How are you going to do that—and how will you receive strength from others—if you go it alone? Attending a small-group meeting with a friend or with your husband will add new energy and purpose to your life in the middle years. You could also seek out a women's group where you can be nurtured in your faith and in turn nurture others.

As a woman who has matured in Christ over the years, you can pass on what you've learned to younger women. Think back on your own struggles during those earlier times—did an older woman help you survive difficult adjustments? Pay attention to women younger than you. Could you be an encouragement and support to them, without giving unasked-for advice?[2]

For spiritual companionship on the journey through mid-life, join other women from your church or contact a few friends and get together to discuss the "Reflection" questions. Profit from your time together by praying and brainstorming on ways to snap out of the spiritual doldrums. Experiencing the reality and passion of your first love *can* happen again.[3]

2. Make Time for Friends

In the Garden of Eden, Adam had everything—even a close friendship with God. But he was still lonely. We are created with a hunger for companionship, to feel that someone cares about us. Current research shows that intimate relationships play a vital role in our well-being, echoing God's words in Genesis 2:18, "It is not good for man (or woman) to be alone." Even though you have a spouse or other close family members, you need friends.

Close Friends Are Vital for Your Well-Being

According to one research poll, "people who could name five close friends were 60 percent more likely to be 'very happy' than those who couldn't."[4] Close friendships help us cope better with bereavement, personal tragedies, and hard times. Being able to pour out your hurt, confusion, or pain to a close and caring friend is free therapy. A friend provides a sounding board for your thoughts and supplies strength to go on.

Cultivating long-term friendships and establishing newer ones does take time, but consider: you'll not only have fun and companionship now, you'll also have someone to share tomorrow's unknowns with. If you're married, statistics say you will outlive your husband. Then who will share your life?

Assess and Nurture Your Friendships

Now is the time to look at your friendships with other women. How many are close and supportive? Which have you neglected for whatever reasons—are they ones you could revive with a little effort on your part? Make contact, take the risk of reestablishing a relationship. Or, when you meet someone you'd like to get to know, invite them to do something with you. While you're at it, think about what kind of friend you are.

Intimate friendships are not only soul-satisfying, they help guarantee a healthy life. To add zest and vitality to your years, you need more than megadoses of multivitamins or regular workouts at the gym: you need to expand and deepen your circle of friends.

3. Take Care of Yourself

To thrive in the middle years and beyond doesn't mean you should live your life like a video permanently stuck on fast-forward. For well-being, make time for solitude and sufficient sleep, something that is usually missing when life zips by in a blur.

Take Time to Be Quiet

"Come with me by yourselves to a quiet place and get some rest," said Jesus to his weary disciples, knowing that if they didn't, they would fall apart. He also said, "Come to me, all you who are weary and burdened, and I will give you rest." The need for quietness as a counterbalance to busy lives is a theme clearly woven through Scripture.[5] We ignore it to our peril.

What warning signs signal your energy gauge is on empty? Consider the following: an innocent request sends you over the edge. You spend all day trying to figure out how to keep going. Despite working frantically, your "to do" list keeps growing. You have no time for family, friends, or yourself. You groan every time the phone rings. You have no desire to show compassion or caring to others. You feel particularly vulnerable to temptation.

To thrive means getting quiet and giving regular attention to what's going on inside you. To do that, spend some time in introspection, praying for God to show you which activities and attitudes in your life are good and which are harmful. Think about your relationships. Do the ones that leave you feeling drained outnumber those that build you up? What can you do to change the ratio? Reflect on your goals, your motives, and dreams. Also look closely at your eating, sleeping, and exercise patterns. Do these contribute to your well-being, or do you need to take yourself by the scruff of the neck and make some lifestyle changes?

Refill Your Emotional Tank

Begin to identify all the ways you can think of that replenish you emotionally—maybe exploring a different part of town, buying a new kind of magazine, making a long-distance call to a friend you rarely talk to, splurging on tickets to a concert, indulging in a massage. Make up your own list of what would renew you, then put at least one on your schedule every week.

Take care of yourself at this season of life by recharging your batteries on a regular basis. After all, you give your car regular tune-ups, don't you? Isn't it wise to also give yourself a little tender loving care?

4. Live at Your Own Pace

Remember the old saying, "All work and no play makes Jack a dull boy"? Not only does it make Jack a dull boy, it can drive even the hardest-charging Jill to burnout.

In addition to tuning in to what's going on inside you and scheduling personal renewal and nurturing times, thriving comes from establishing a sane pace of life.

Monitor Your Energy Level

To have time and energy for what is important to you, pay attention to your personal energy level—both physically and emotionally. If you're constantly pushing yourself to the brink of exhaustion, ask yourself why.

Without realizing what's happening, life can become like an over-stuffed suitcase, packed beyond reason with your own or someone else's expectations or demands. Let's be honest—overly full lives get that way for many reasons: as a consequence of going through a season of greater than normal demands, as a way to avoid time to think and feel, as an effort to quench a thirst for approval and applause.

Whatever the reason for living beyond your normal energy level, ultimately the effects of adrenaline wear off. Then, instead of thriving, you find yourself barely surviving.

Evaluate Your Lifestyle

If life seems out of control, ask yourself, "What importance will this activity have a year from now, or five years from now, or from the perspective of eternity?"

Take a fresh look at your priorities during these middle years and learn to say no without guilt and inner recriminations. Select realistic goals for yourself, then begin to accomplish them at your own speed. You're not in a race against anyone. By breaking even the largest task into small, daily, personally doable steps, you can enjoy the process as well as the results.

An effective and fulfilling life is possible without an over-crowded appointment book, racing from one "must do" activity to another, or fuming at every red traffic light. Savor quality time over a busy schedule and determine to live at a pace that is sane for you. In the final analysis, does it really matter that your been-there-done-that list is shorter than someone else's?

5. Move Your Body

Peeping around the door at a class full of silver-haired women vigorously engaged in step aerobics, my amazement turned to admiration. Wanting to sample an over-forties class, I slid into a space in the back row and joined in enthusiastically—for about fifteen minutes. *I have to be the youngest person in this group*, I thought, *but how come I'm the one gasping for breath while they merrily prance around?*

Without regular exercise, we get stiffer and slower as we age. Before making exercise a habit, I found it wasn't just the bed that creaked in the mornings. Turning my neck produced grinding noises and bending my knees was the only way I could reach my toes. Despite an ingrained conviction that I'm too young to have an old body, warning lights flashed PAY ATTENTION.

Start Where You Are

As I discovered, you're never too old, or undisciplined, or out-of-shape to begin exercising. In fact, if you're not currently active, you stand to gain the most health benefits from moving your body.

At a minimum, exercise regularly three days a week for 30 minutes. Join a gym, a class, or a friend who works out several times a week. Get a machine and anchor it in front of the TV, then when you watch the news or your favorite program, start moving. Put on exercise togs and your walking shoes first thing in the morning or when you get home. Open the front door and go.

Anticipate the Benefits

Why do we need to work at moving our bodies in the middle years? Because physical activity is another key ingredient in healthy aging. Exercise makes you feel good and releases chemicals that help you battle depression and anxiety.

Getting out of your chair or off the sofa and working out also improves your balance, keeps you flexible, and gives you more stamina. Need more motivation? Ask yourself if you really want to be in a high-risk group for heart disease, elevated blood pressure, and diabetes. Wouldn't you rather put a stop to those creaking and grinding noises, and be able to tie your shoelaces without risking major injury?

6. Keep Learning

When did you last take a class—on anything? What book or article have you read recently that made you think? To feel intensely alive, stay aware of what's happening around you. Feed fresh knowledge and ideas into your mind.

Improve Your Brain Power

Can a flabby mind be improved just like a flabby body? Yes. So discard your fears about losing your mind, not being able to remember facts and figures, and drawing a blank when introducing your best friend.

Researchers on the aging mind declare that mental decline is not inevitable, but rather a result of disuse. The remedy? Give your brain a workout with mental aerobics.

God challenged Adam to use his mental abilities when He told him to name all the animals. He's also given us amazing brains capable of continuous growth and learning, so long as they aren't left on some shelf to gather dust now that we're in mid-life.

Learn and Thrive

Learning doesn't have to be solely for personal advancement. It can be for pleasure. The results are the same: mastering material you feared was beyond you, finding your memory actually gets sharper with greater use, feeling electric with energy as you learn about great painters, ancient civilizations, Chinese cuisine, or how to browse the worldwide web and connect with someone in Nepal. In addition to thriving on new and exciting knowledge, you'll keep your problem-solving skills sharp; your ability to organize your thoughts from going rusty.

If mastering something new is difficult, practice learning to concentrate. Go over the material again and again. Don't give up until you've grasped it. Make your mind work by tackling crossword puzzles or pitting yourself against game show contestants. Conquer that complex DVD machine or new computer program, learn a new hobby, or study something that fascinates you.[6]

Challenge yourself to come up with a dozen ways to stretch your mind by feeding it new information. Start working on your list, and stand back and watch yourself glow with renewed confidence and a zest for living.

7. Choose a Positive Attitude

What's the difference between viewing a situation as an opportunity or seeing it as an obstacle? Attitude. Choosing your attitude is the single most important daily decision you make.

Attitude Determines Success

Deciding whether to go for your dreams, to try again, to attempt what seems beyond you is all a matter of attitude. A positive attitude, not circumstances, makes you more open to new opportunities and determines your level of fulfillment in your second adult life-span.

However, no matter what you attempt to achieve, worthwhile accomplishments don't usually happen without going through three distinct stages: *It's impossible. It's difficult. It's done.*

Without a positive I CAN attitude, the temptation is to stop at the first thought of *It's impossible.* Giving up before you start, or withering at the first difficulty, wipes out even the possibility of saying, "It's done." As one observer of life said, "If you're waiting for your ship to come in, you must first send it out."

Attitude Influences Outlook

One of the dangers as we grow older is becoming negative and rigid in our response to people and circumstances.

When this happens, we lose our openness to new approaches or considering the possibility of change in others, ourselves, or our circumstances.

How do we avoid this emotional dead end and cultivate a happy and positive attitude? A good place to start is found in Paul's letter to the Philippians: Focus on what's true, right, and good.[7] In other words, pay attention to what is positive in others, in yourself, and in the situations you face. Even obstacles have hidden opportunities for growth. Look for them; you'll find them.

It takes discipline to catch those negative thoughts that surge into your mind when tough or disheartening situations arise, but you can do it. Choose to consciously think about what is truthful and what is positive, even if you must struggle to do so.

As you think positive and encouraging thoughts, verbalize them to others. Your family, the person you work alongside, your neighbor, all need building up. By your cheery attitude you may help them "go and do likewise."

Practice a positive attitude in your prayer time also. Instead of moaning and groaning to God about your problems, pray positively. Express your faith in God, and ask Him to help you think and speak positively to others as well as to yourself.

You can make life easier or harder by the attitude you choose to adopt every day. Negative emotions, a grumpy attitude, and a pessimistic outlook on life will drain away your joy.

You don't have to pretend life is perfect to wake up each morning and begin the day by counting your blessings. Lift your spirits by keeping a mental tally every day of all the pleasurable things that happen: a yummy lunch, a hug from a friend, store coupons for just those items you need, buying shoes that not only look great but are comfortable.

A positive attitude lightens your heart and puts a sparkle on your face, causing others to enjoy being around you. Develop a good habit by making it a daily choice.

8. Engage in Work That Matters to You

For emotional health, we all need to be engaged in some form of productive work. If the highlight of your day is waiting for the mailman to arrive, a change in your routine may be overdue.

God created us with a desire to use our lives in a useful manner. Without this occupation, we become listless, bored, and depressed. Those studying the elderly in nursing homes found that even the stimulus of caring for a plant provided a reason for living.

Having structure in our lives, something to do on a regular basis that matters to us, fuels the feeling that life is good.

Work is a gift from God, not something to be avoided. Having made us, God knows that doing something productive increases our sense of self-worth, brings satisfaction and fulfillment, and gives a feeling of pride and pleasure in being useful and needed.

Whatever work you do, whether it's completing your household chores, fixing a good meal, running a business, or teaching computer skills or a Bible study, being engaged in something productive is vital for a thriving life.

At the age of sixty, Cecilia Hurwich did her master's thesis on *Vital Women in Their Seventies and Eighties*. She discovered that the key to growth, change, and vitality shared by these women was a refusal to conform to the stereotype of "little old ladies." Rejecting stagnant and boring lives, they chose to be risk-takers, adapting positively to life's inevitable changes and staying vitally connected to the present.[8] The key to your growth in mid-life is the same.

As women in the sometimes muddled middle years, don't settle for merely surviving. Make it your aim to thrive.

By the way, have you ever wondered how old you'll look in heaven? Just imagine being able to cheerfully say for all eternity, "Yes, I know I look too young to be this old."

Notes

Chapter 1 What's Happening to Me?

1. Ronald Mantieimer, PhD, *The Second Middle Age* (Visible Ink, 1995), 275.

2. Proverbs 3:5–6.

3. Quoted in an article by Melinda Beck, "The New Middle-Age," *Newsweek* (December 7, 1992), 50–56.

4. *Good Housekeeping* (January 1992), 76.

5. *Utne Reader* (January/February 1990), 73. Excerpted from Jeremy Baker, *Tolstoy's Bicycle* (St. Martin's Press, Inc.).

6. John 10:10.

Chapter 2 Everything Seems to Be Changing

1. W. Bridges, *Transitions* (Addison-Wesley, 1980).

2. Ruth 1:16.

3. Matthew 11:28; 1 Peter 4:19.

4. Isaiah 26:3.

5. Robert S. Eliot, MD, *From Stress to Strength* (Bantam, 1994).

6. Romans 8:28; Matthew 16:18; Matthew 25:14–21.

7. Philippians 4:19.

8. Philippians 2:13.

9. James 1:22–25.

Chapter 3 Who *Is* That in the Mirror?

1. Psalm 139:14; 1 Corinthians 6:19–20.
2. Robert G. Wells, MD, and Mary C. Wells, *Menopause and Mid-life* (Tyndale House, 1990).
3. 2 Corinthians 4:16.
4. Proverbs 31:30.
5. Colossians 3:1–2.
6. John 5:24; 6:40, 47.

Chapter 4 "Will You Still Love Me When I'm . . . ?"

1. University of Chicago research, quoted in article by William R. Mattox Jr., in *Focus on the Family* (April 1996).
2. Sonya Rhodes, PhD, *Second Honeymoon* (New York: W. Morrow, 1992).
3. Proverbs 14:1.
4. Doug and Joyce Wachsmuth, 11424 S.W. 47th Ave., Portland, OR 97219.
5. Deborah Tannen, PhD, *You Just Don't Understand* (New York: W. Morrow, 1990).
6. Malachi 2:13–16.
7. Matthew 7:12.

Chapter 5 These Children Are Too Old to Be Mine

1. William and Candace Backus, *What Did I Do Wrong?* (Minneapolis: Bethany House Publishers, 1990). Other helpful resources include John White, *Parents in Pain* (InterVarsity Press, 1979); Jerry and Mary White, *When Your Kids Aren't Kids Anymore* (Navpress, 1989); L. Ashner and M. Meyerson, *When Parents Love Too Much* (New York: William Morrow & Co., 1990); Quentin F. & Emmy Lou Schenk, *Pulling Up Roots* (Prentice Hall, Spectrum Books, 1978).
2. Gary R. Collins, PhD, *Christian Counseling* (Word Books, 1980), 220–23.
3. Proverbs 15:1.
4. 2 Corinthians 1:21–22; Philippians 1:6; 1 Thessalonians 5:23–24.
5. 1 Samuel 16:7.

Chapter 6 My Parents Need Me—How Should I Help?

1. AARP, 601 E. St. N.W., Washington, DC 20049.

2. Living Will: Tells a doctor that you do not want your life artificially prolonged under certain circumstances.

3. Advance Medical Directive: In some states there is an important difference between this document and a living will. Both need two witnesses. Check your state's legal requirements regarding both of these documents.

4. Luke 14:28–33.

5. Isaiah 40:29–31.

6. Isaiah 55:8–9.

7. Patricia Rushford, *The Help, Hope, and Cope Book* (Revell, 1985).

8. Care Facilities: Contact The American Association of Homes for the Aging, 901 E. St. N.W., Suite 500, Washington, DC 20004-2037, for helpful resources. Also contact: Assisted Living Facility Association of America, 9401 Lee Highway, Ste. 402, Fairfax, VA 22031.

Chapter 7 If Only I Had . . . or Hadn't

1. David A. Seamands and Beth Funk, *Healing for Damaged Emotions Workbook* (Victor Books, 1992). Other helpful resources: Ron Lee Davis, *Mistreated* (Multnomah Press, 1989); Beverly Flanigan, *Forgiving the Unforgivable* (McMillan, 1992).

2. Galatians 5:2–23.

3. Philippians 3:12–14.

4. Genesis 50:20.

5. Romans 12:21; Ephesians 4:31–32; Colossians 3:13.

6. Psalm 103:8–14.

7. Matthew 11:28; 2 Corinthians 1:3–4; Ephesians 3:20; Jeremiah 29:11.

Chapter 8 I Can't Do That . . . or Can I?

1. Gail Sheehy, *New Passages: Mapping Your Life Across Time* (Random House, 1995).

2. Matthew 25:14–27; 1 Corinthians 12:4–11; Ephesians 2:10; John 10:10.

3. Exodus 3–4:17; Numbers 13:26–14:24; Jeremiah 1:4–19.

4. 1 Peter 5:8–9.

5. David Burns, MD, *Feeling Good: The New Mood Therapy* (New York: Signet, 1980).

6. To learn more about the power of self-talk see: William Backus and Marie Chapian, *Telling Yourself the Truth* (Minneapolis: Bethany House Publishers, 1980).

7. Psalm 42:5.

8. Psalm 17:8; Isaiah 41:8–10; 43:4; Ephesians 1:1–14; 1 John 3:1.

9. Jan Mitchell, *The Sunday Oregonian* (Nov. 5, 1989).

10. James 1:22–25.

Chapter 9 Who Am I, Now That I've Grown Up?

1. Ruth McRoberts Ward, *Self-Esteem, A Gift from God* (Baker Books, 1984).

2. *Puzzles, Patterns, and Pathways*, University of Arizona. Adapted by permission, New Directions Program, Portland Community College, Portland, Oregon. 1986.

3. Betty Neville Michelozzi, *Coming Alive From Nine to Five, the Career Search Handbook*, third edition (Mayfield Publishing Co., 1988), 84.

4. Ibid. 94–95.

5. *Puzzles, Patterns, and Pathways*.

6. Ibid.

Chapter 10 Where Do I Go From Here?

1. Matthew 6:33; Colossians 3:1.

2. Romans 12:4–8; 1 Corinthians 12:4–7; Ephesians 4:11–13.

3. For helpful resources, see: *Houts' Inventory of Spiritual Gifts* (Fuller Evangelistic Association, 1985); *Biblical Personal Profiles* (Performax Systems Intl., Inc., USA, 1985); Marcia L. Mitchell, *Giftedness: Discovering Your Areas of Strength* (Minneapolis: Bethany House Publishers, 1988).

4. Bob Shank, *Total Life Management* (Multnomah Press, 1990).

5. Ibid., 30.

6. John 4:34; 5:30; 17:4.

7. Bob Shank, *Total Life Management*, 74–75.

8. James 4:13–15; Proverbs 27:1.

9. Adapted from *Goal Setting and Productivity*, Kathy Edwards (Paulson, Edwards & Assoc., Gresham, Ore.).

10. *Puzzles, Patterns, and Pathways*, 58.

11. Ibid., 115.

Chapter 11 How Do I Get Ready for Being *Really* Old?

1. Bettye Gill and John Clyde, *Solving the Puzzle of Retirement Planning*, 1992, Oregon Retirement Planning Services, 4263 Elf Ave. S.E., Salem, OR 97302.

2. Tom and Nancy Biracree, *Over Fifty: The Resource Book for the Better Half of Your Life* (Harper Perennial, 1991), 3–5.

3. Ibid., 6–121.

4. Penelope Wang, "How to Live Worry-Free When You Retire," *Money* magazine, (November 1996), 166–74.

5. Don and Renee Martin, *A Survival Kit for Wives: How to Avoid Financial Chaos Before Tragedy Strikes* (New York: Villard Books, 1986).

6. Biracree, 284–85.

7. Ibid., 292–96.

8. Foster W. Cline, MD, and Jim Fay, *Grandparenting With Love and Logic* (The Love and Logic Press, Inc., 1994), 9–14.

9. Ibid., 157.

10. Contact ROCKING/Raising Our Children's Kids: (616) 683-9038; AARP Grandparent Information Center: (202)434-2296.

Chapter 12 I'm Not Just Surviving, I'm Thriving

1. George Gallup survey on the "State of Religion in America," quoted by Jeremy Daniel. "Can You Pass the Happiness Test?" *Family Circle* (July 16, 1996), 36–43.

2. Titus 2:3–5.

3. Revelation 2:2–4.

4. Jeremy Daniel, 43.

5. Genesis 2:2–3; Exodus 31:15; 33:14; Psalms 23:1–2; 46:10; Mark 6:31; Matthew 11:28.

6. Alice Lake, "Make Yourself Smarter with Mental Aerobics," *Woman's Day* (November 24, 1987), 50–52.

7. Philippians 4:8–9.

8. Betty Friedan, "Why Women Age Longer and Better Than Men," *Good Housekeeping* (October 1993), 70.

Acknowledgments

I owe a great debt to many older women who have deeply influenced my life through their vibrant love for Jesus Christ. In particular, I wish to thank my spiritual mother, Hilda Matthews of Chester, England, for her loving input during my difficult early years in America. Her many letters, filled with strong counsel, constantly challenged me to a deeper relationship with Jesus Christ. My prayer is that I, too, will be God's voice of encouragement to other women.

I also want to thank Mike Hamil, formerly of Interest Ministries, for being the first to urge me to write what I teach. When others kept saying the same thing, I finally started listening.

Lastly, I want to express my gratitude to Connie Soth for her editorial help. As a sharp, snowy-haired seventy-something, Connie taught me much in the hours we spent together. In addition, she ably demonstrated the theme of this book, that life is to be lived to the full no matter how old we are.

Patricia "Poppy" Smith was for years a Bible Study Fellowship lecturer and is a popular speaker at retreats, conferences, and workshops around the world. Born in England, she has lived in Sri Lanka, Singapore, and Kenya, where she met her American physician husband. They have two grown children.

You can contact Poppy at:

16124 NW St. Andrews Drive
Portland, OR 97229

A practical and inspiring guide *for women* approaching menopause.

The Menopause Guide challenges old myths and provides practical solutions so women can embrace this dynamic and positive season of life.

a division of Baker Publishing Group
www.RevellBooks.com

Available at your local bookstore